Songwriting Journal

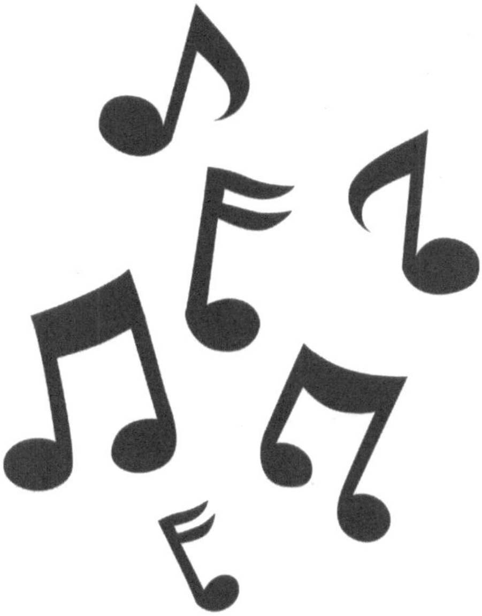

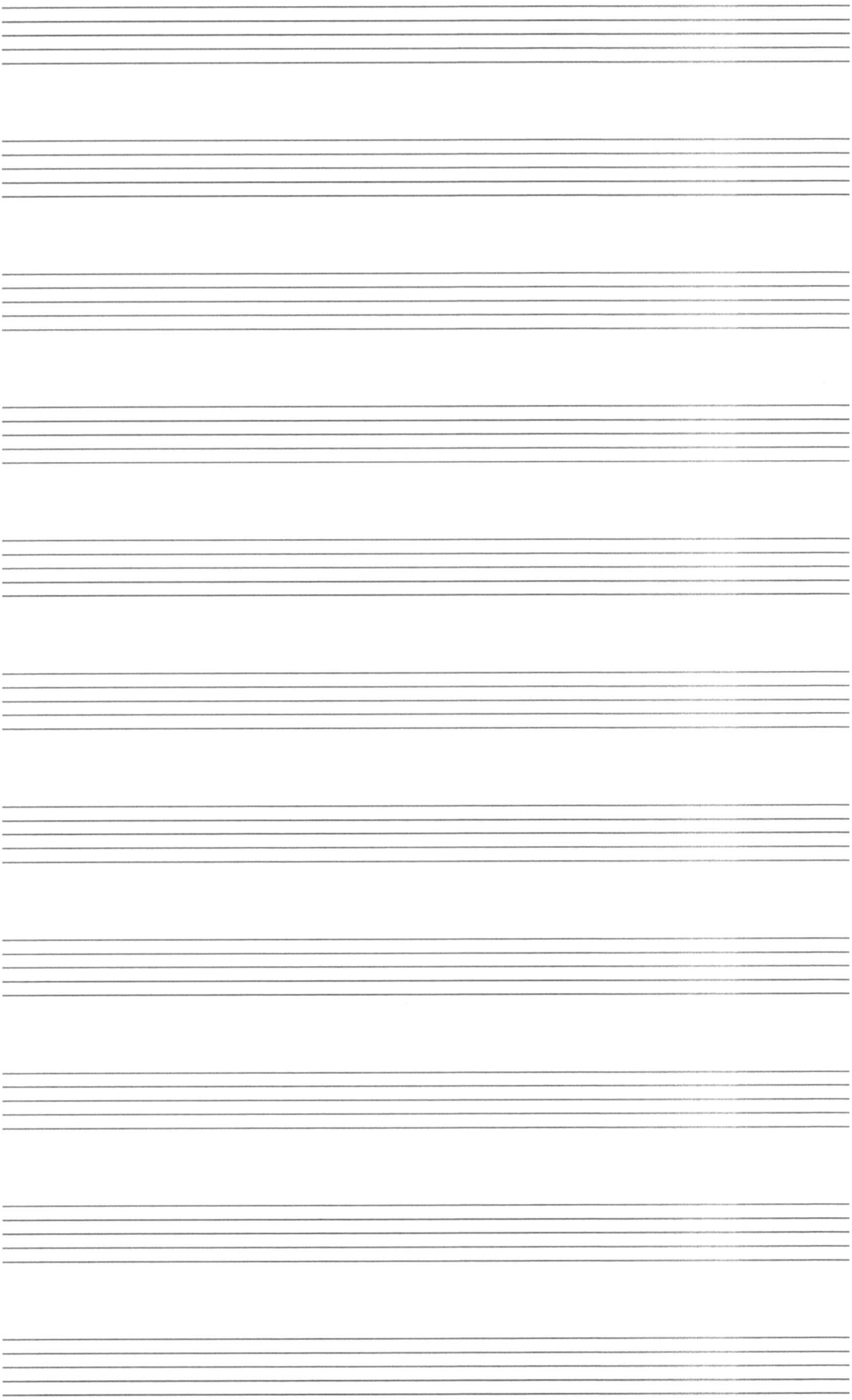

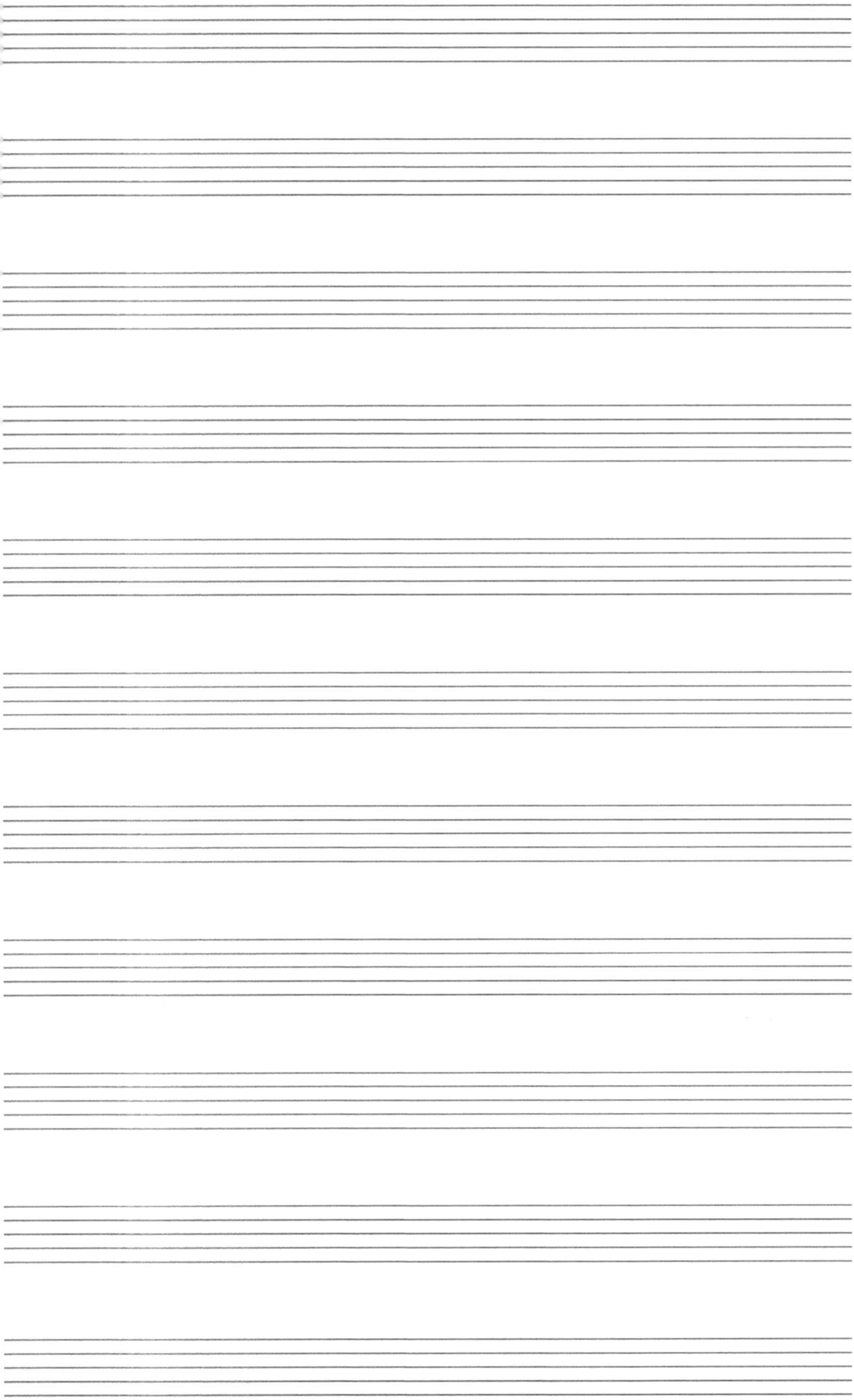

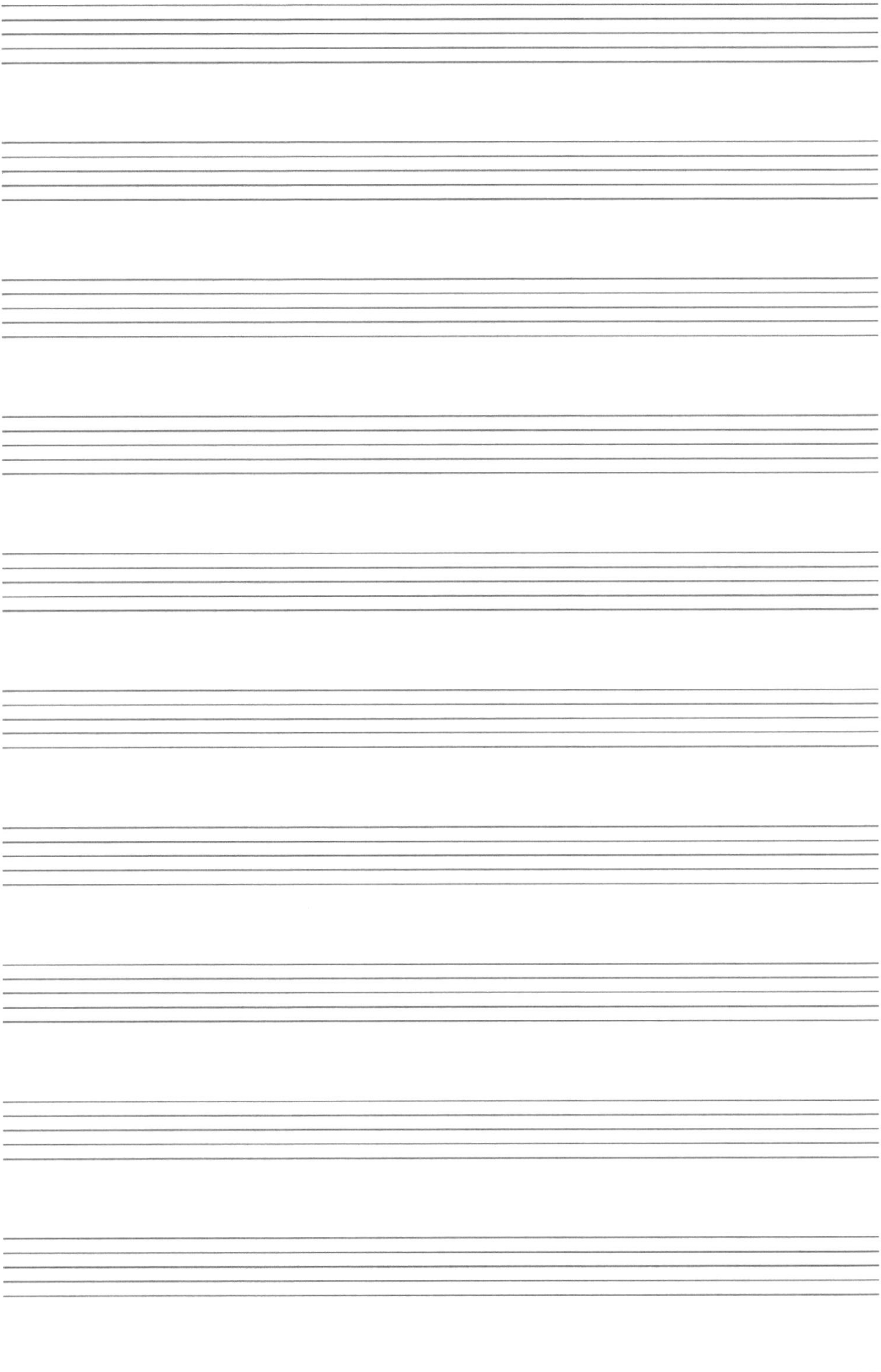

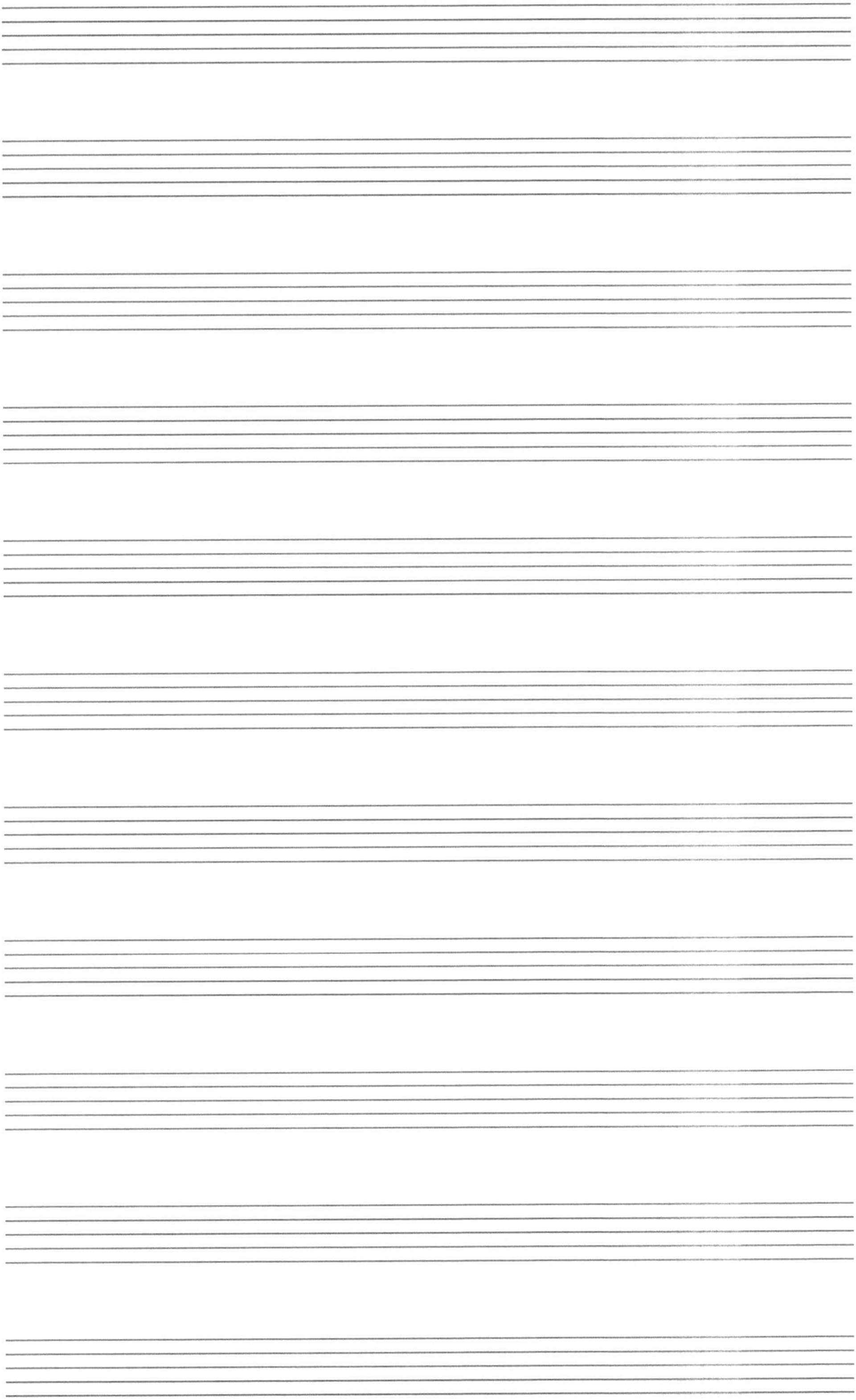

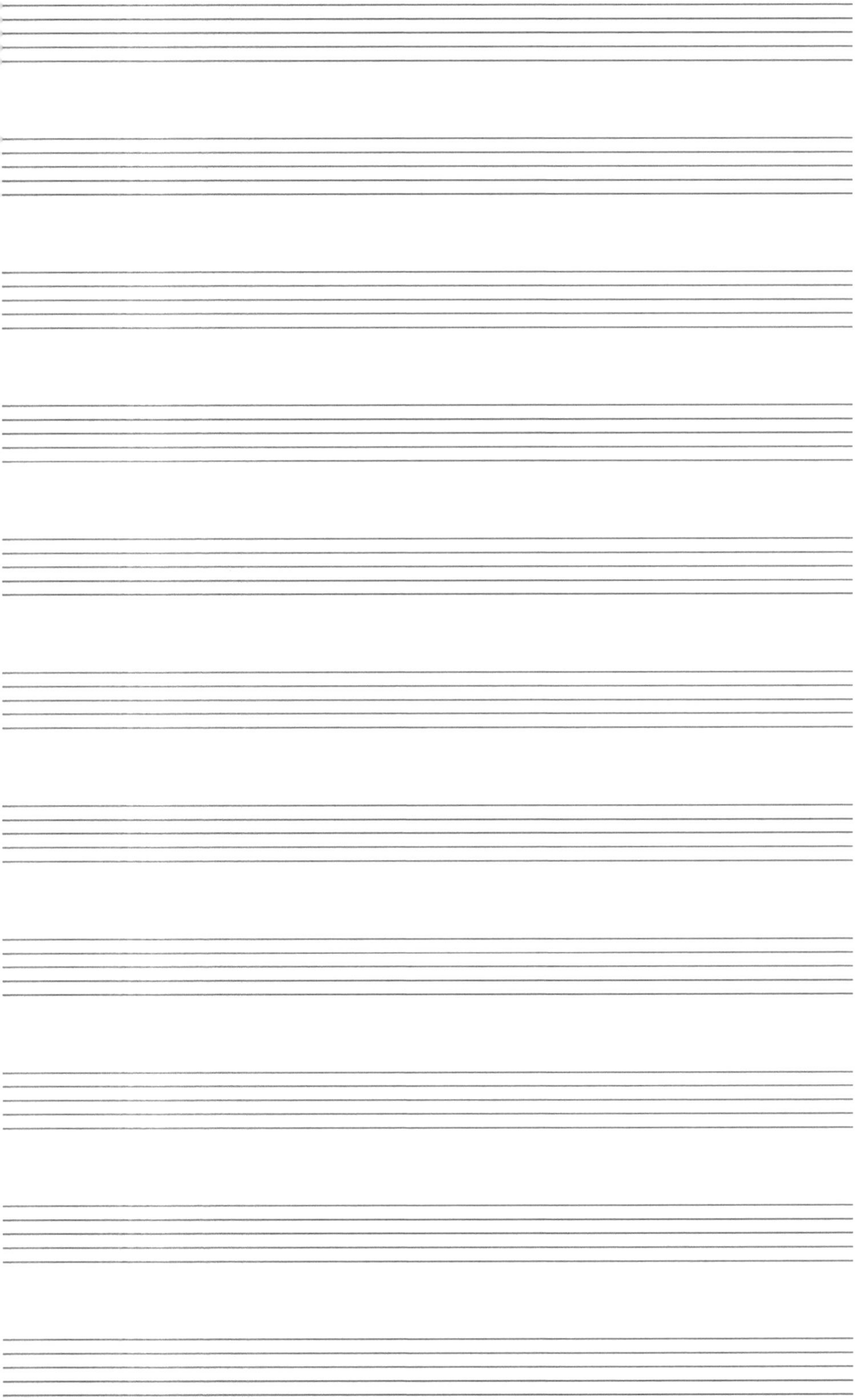

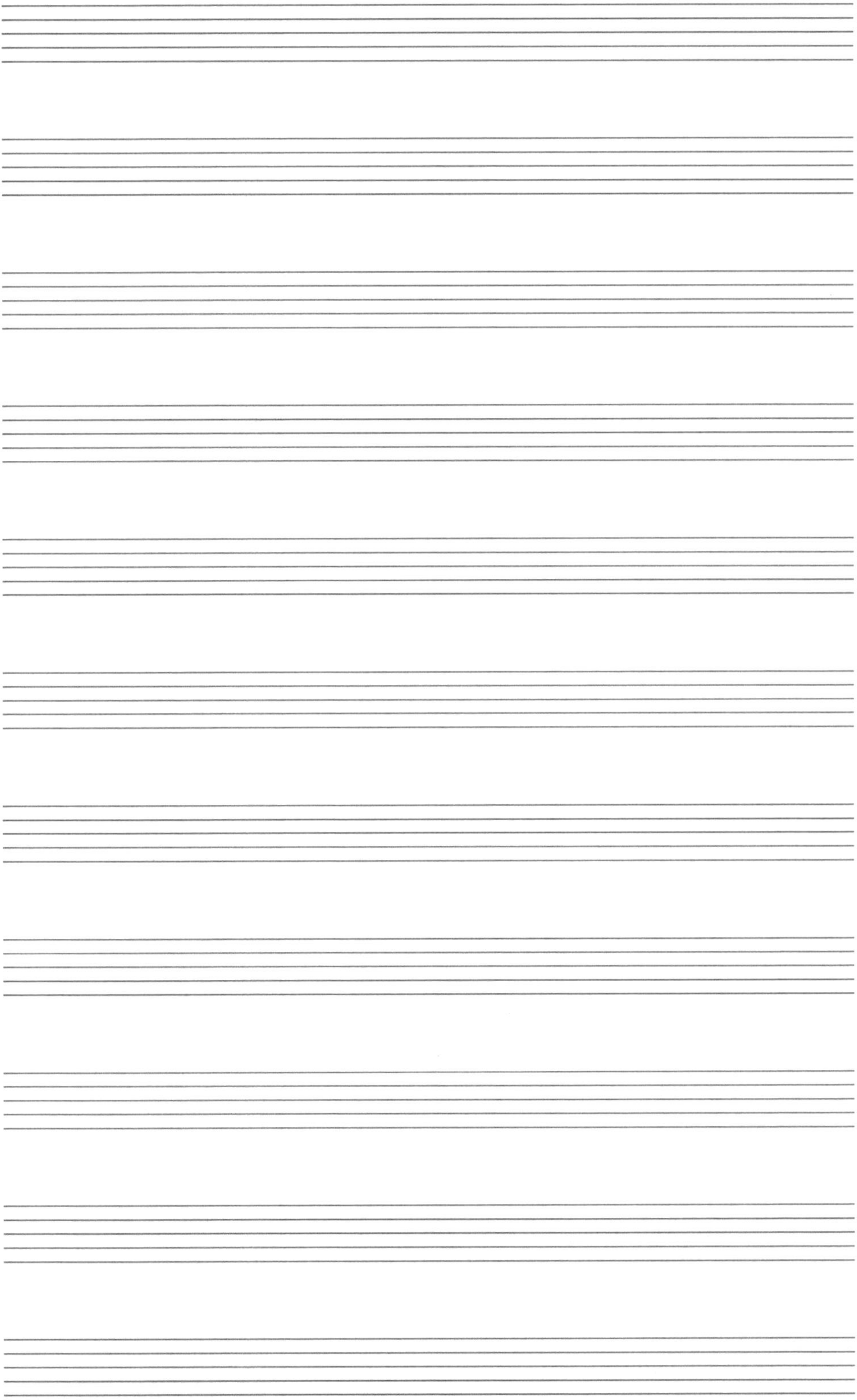

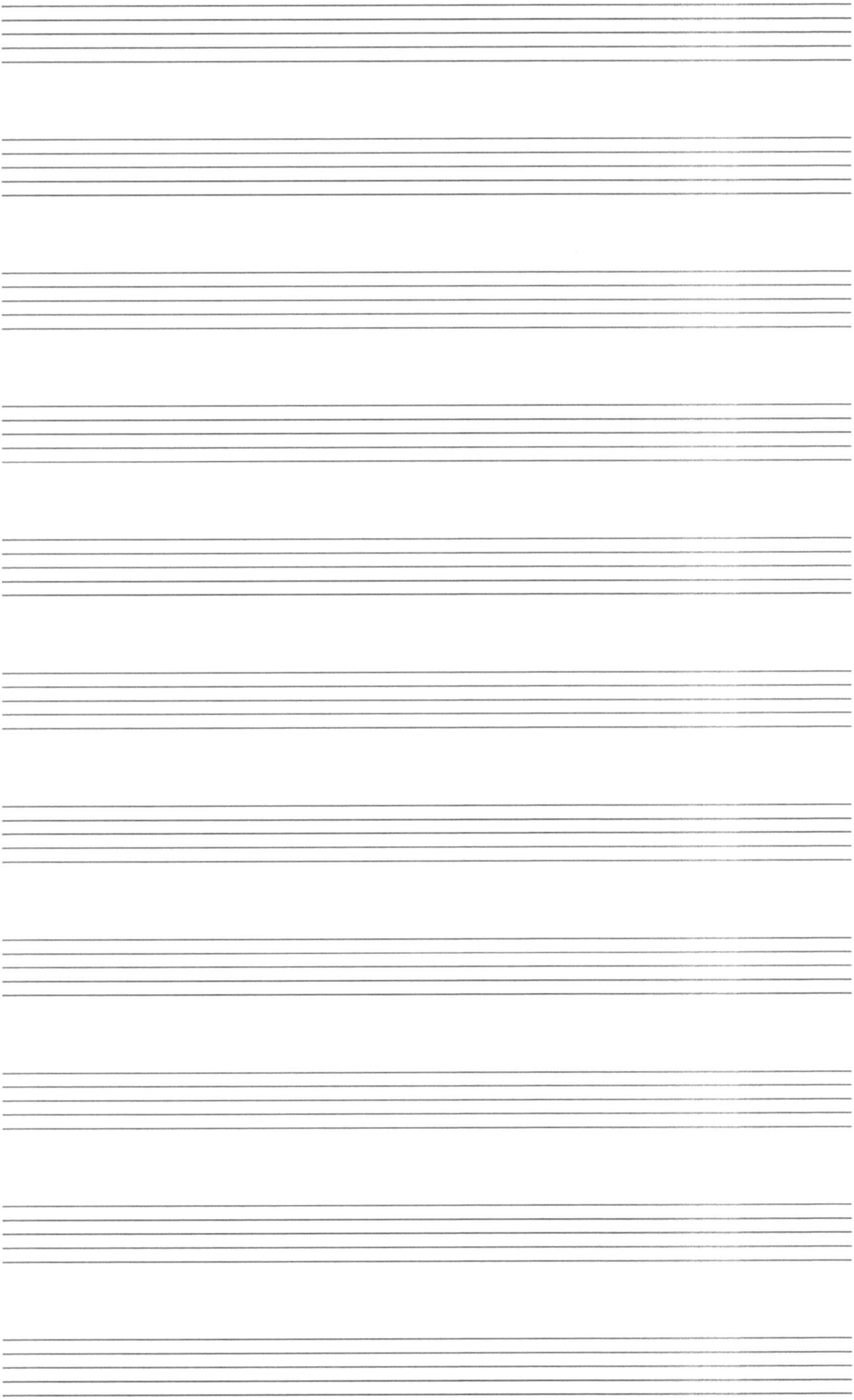

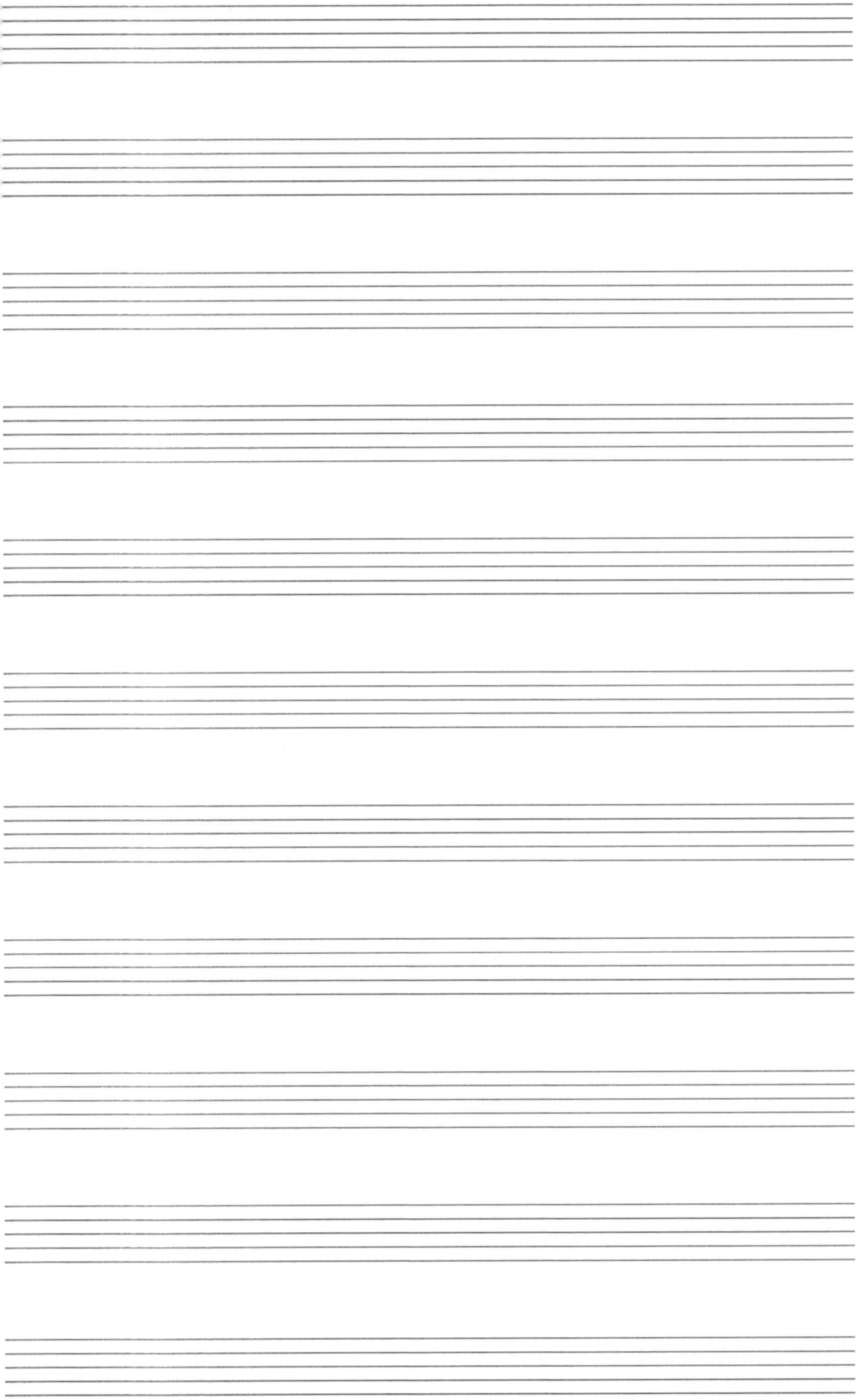

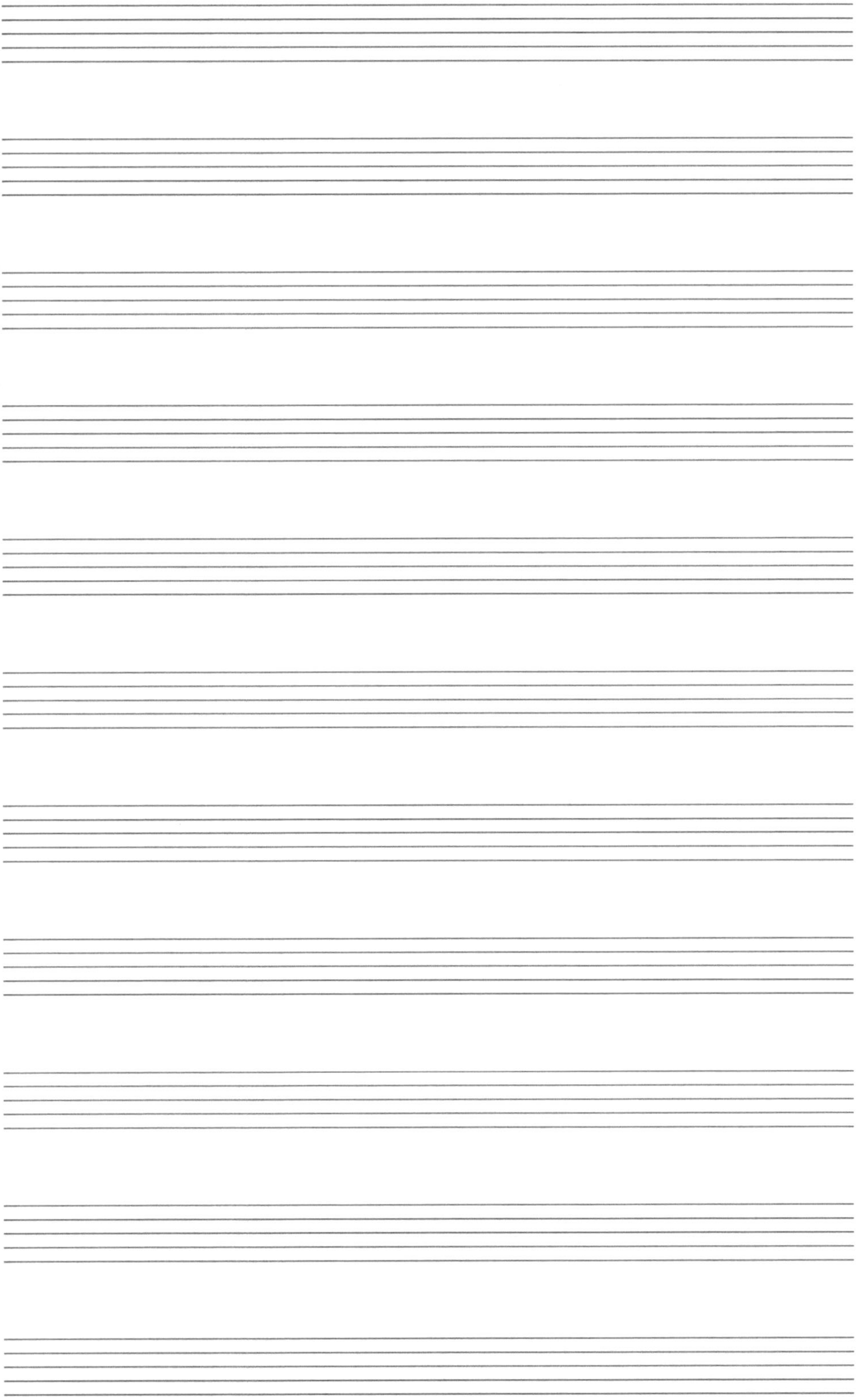

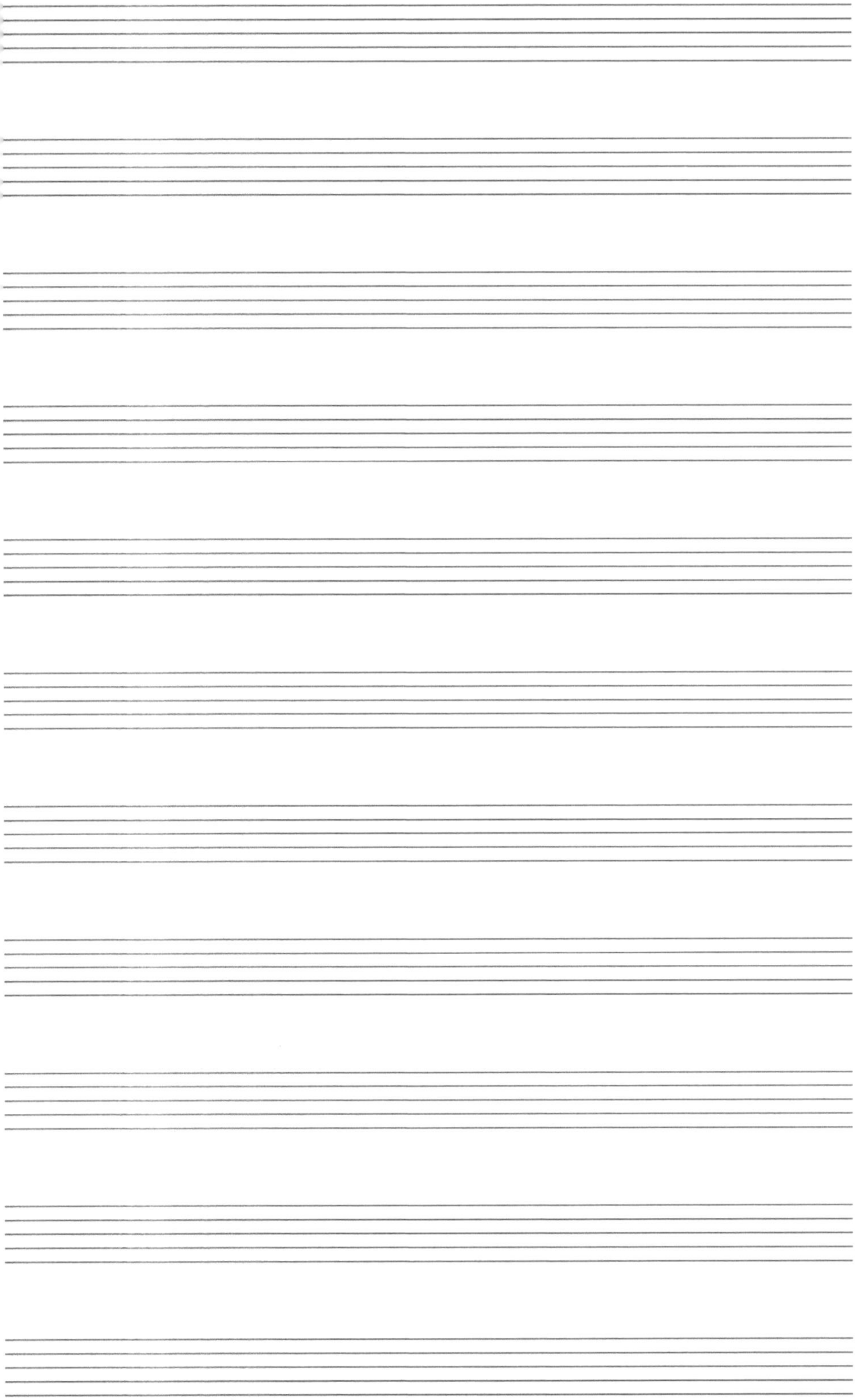

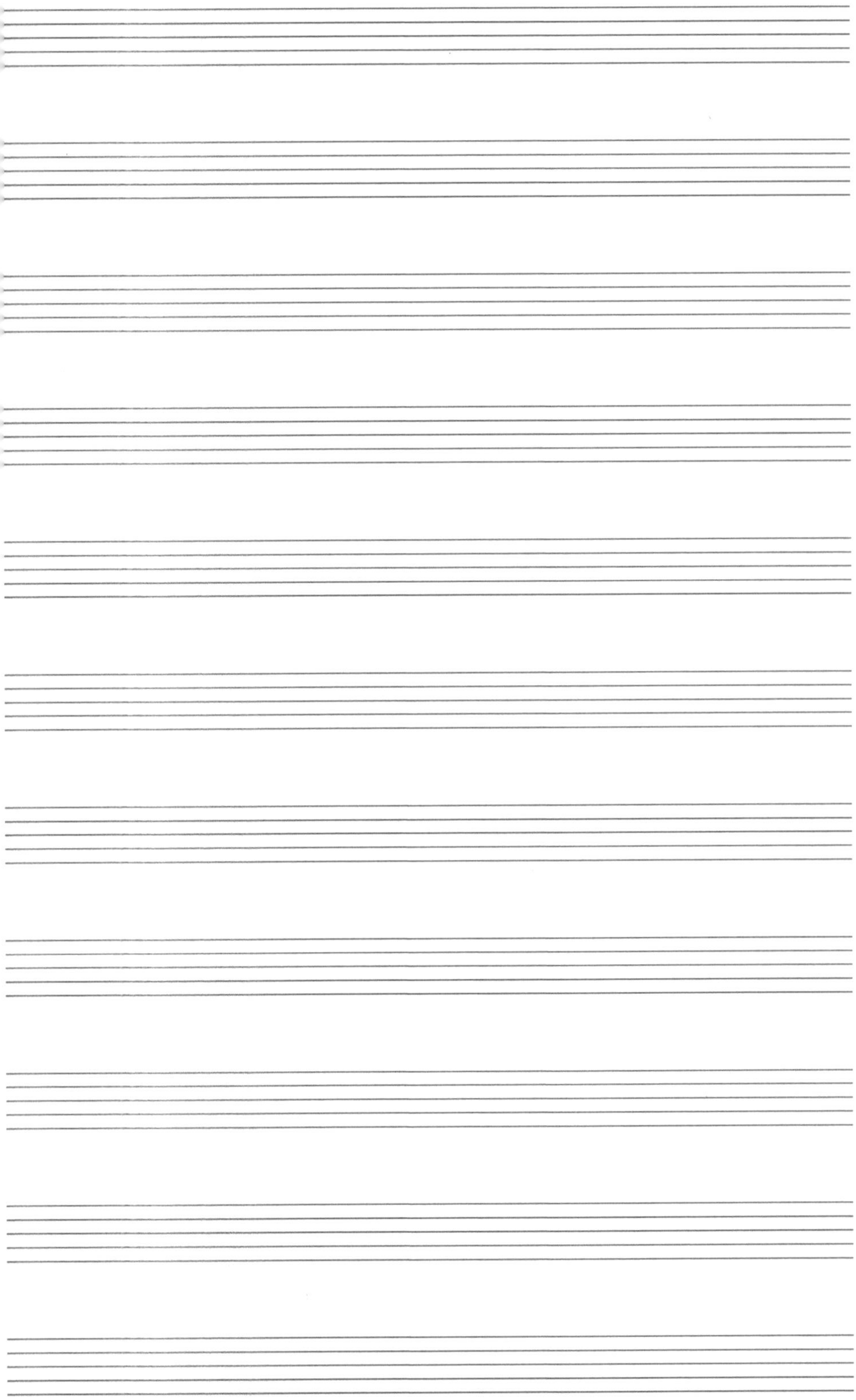

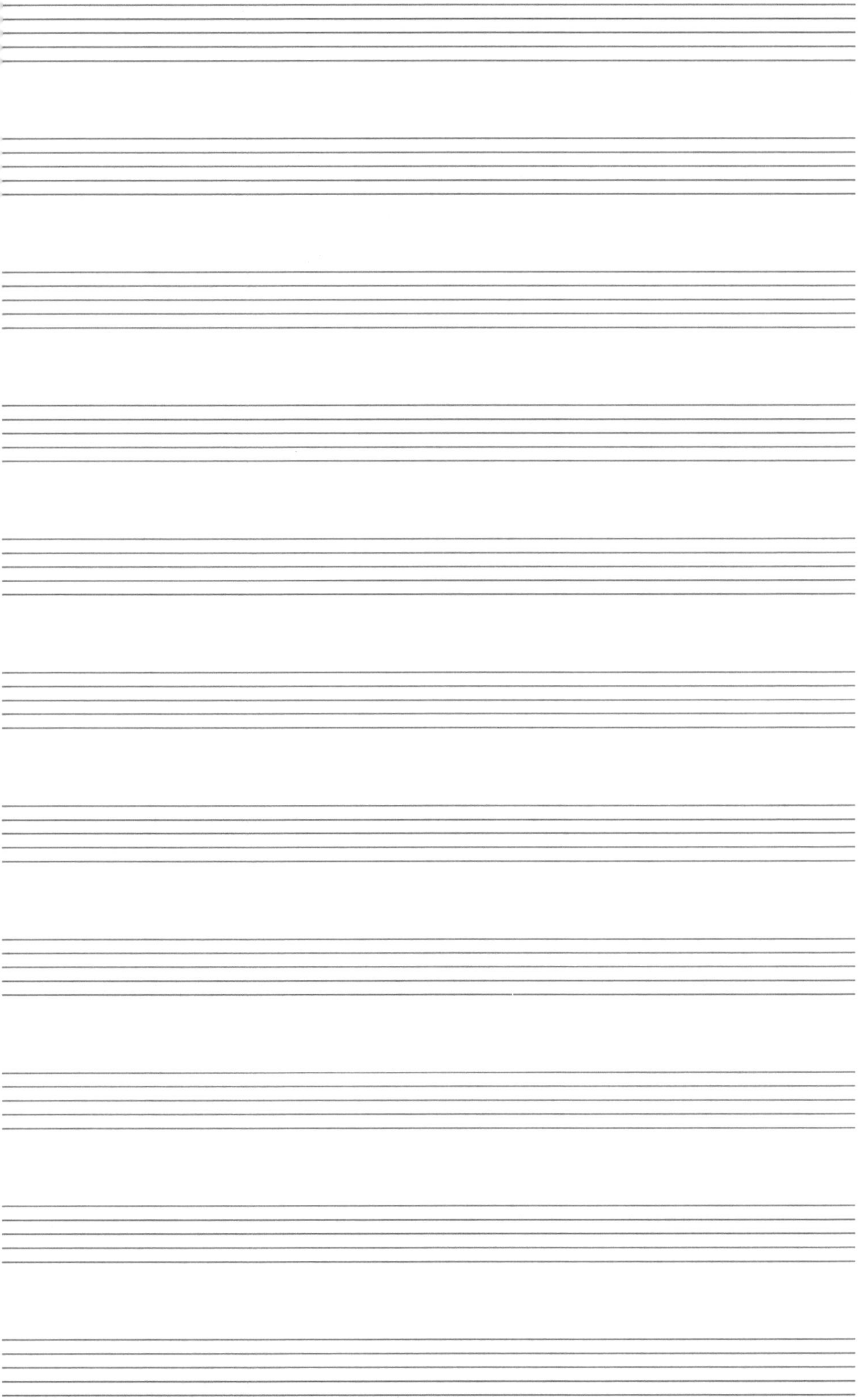

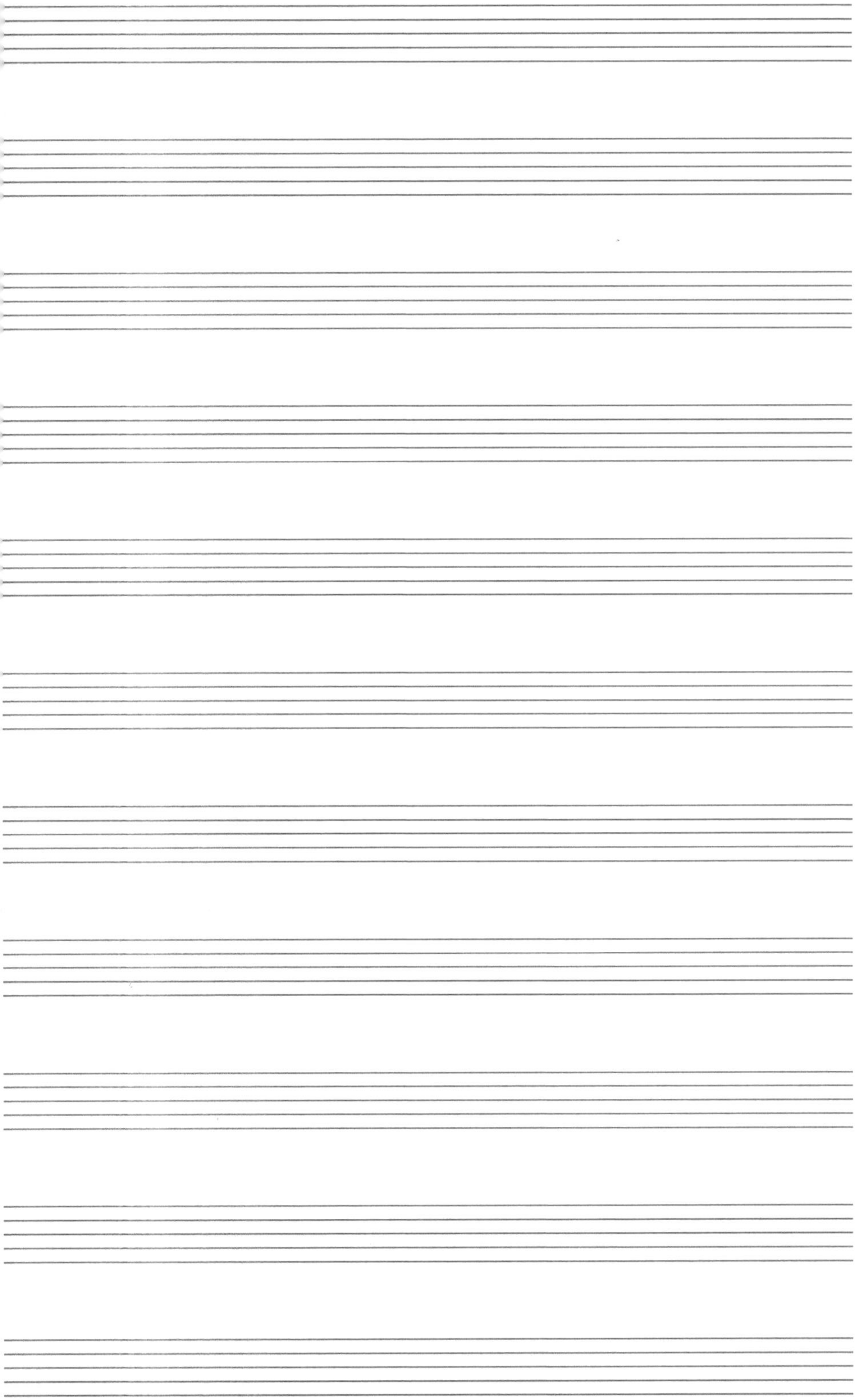

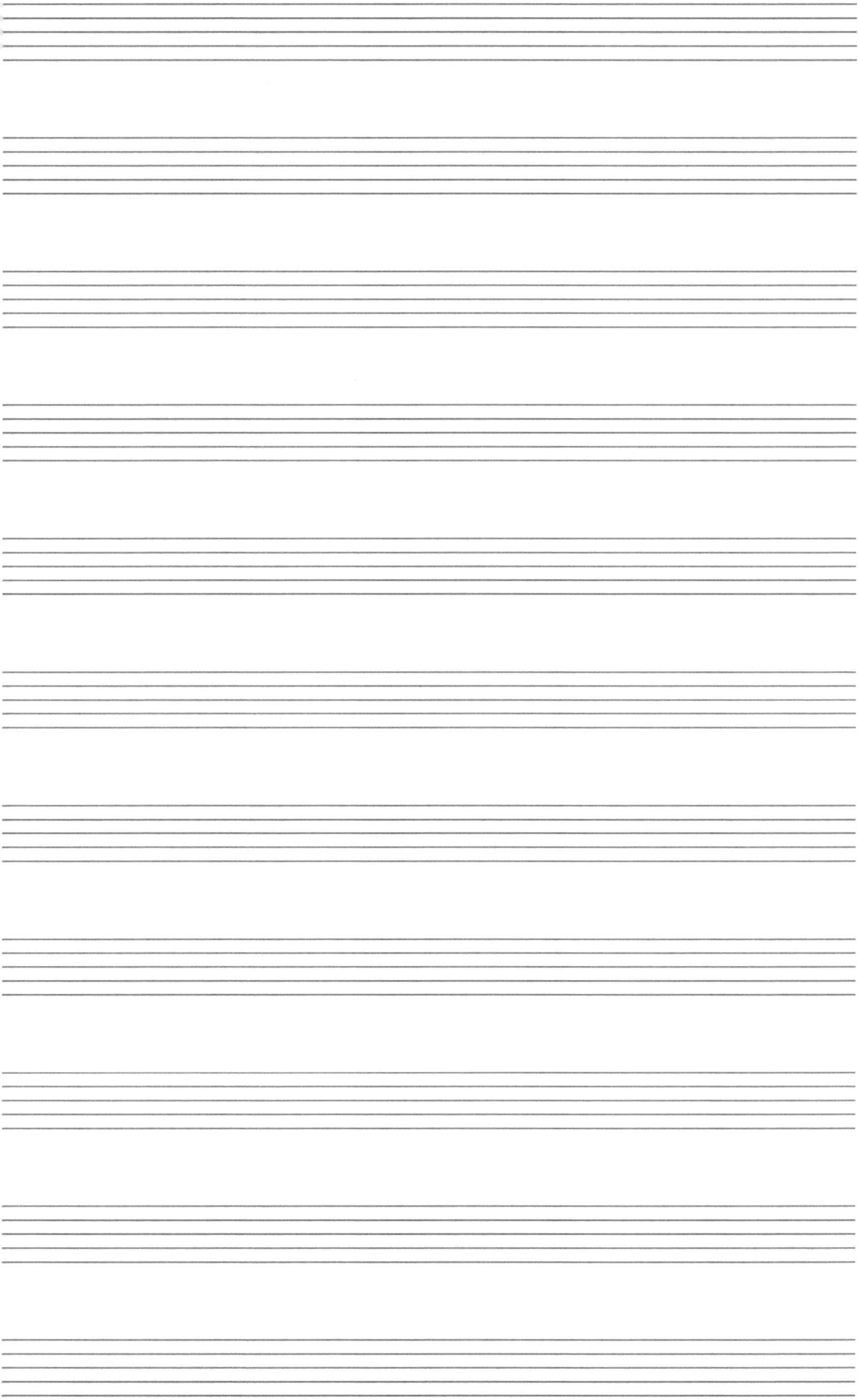

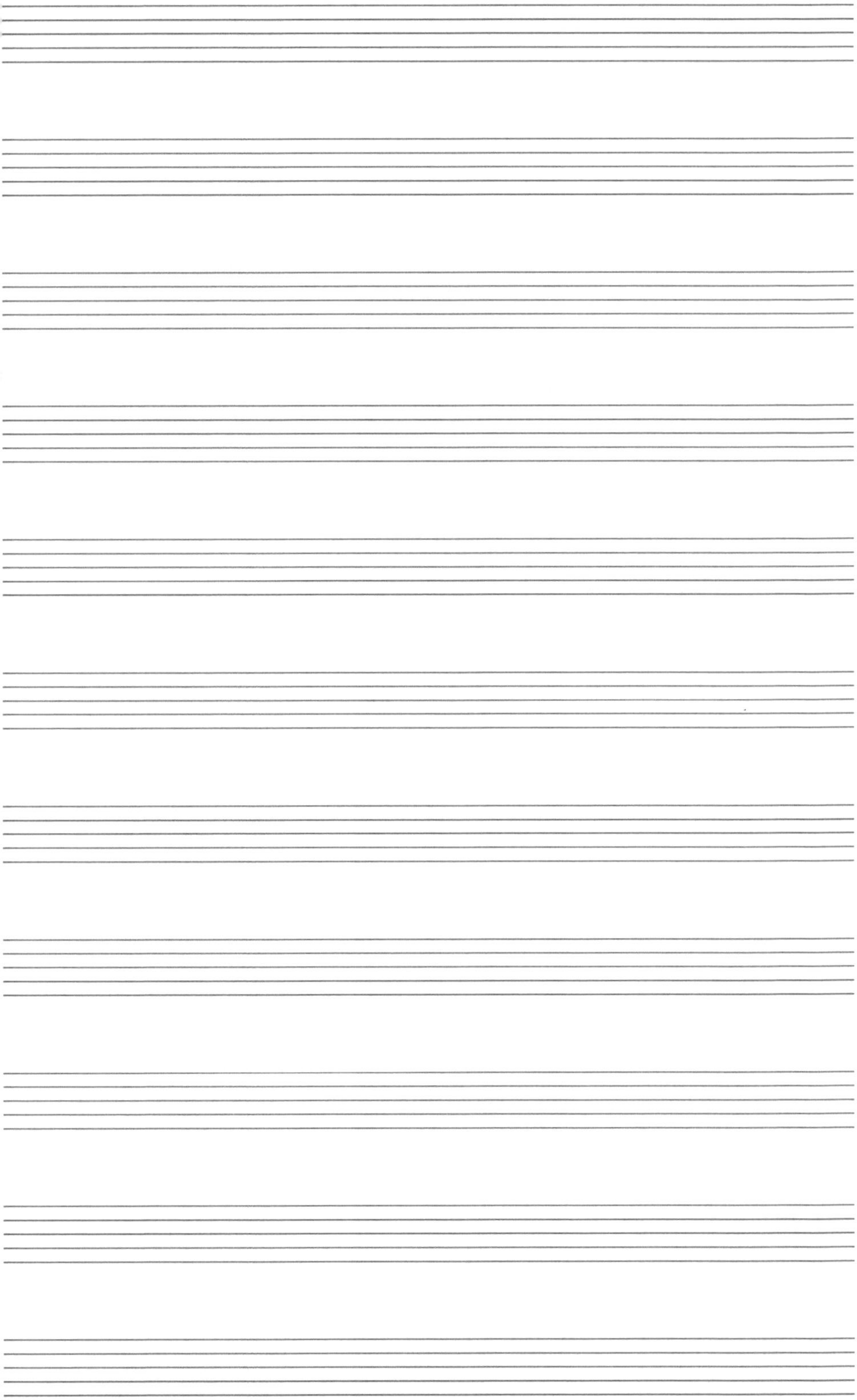

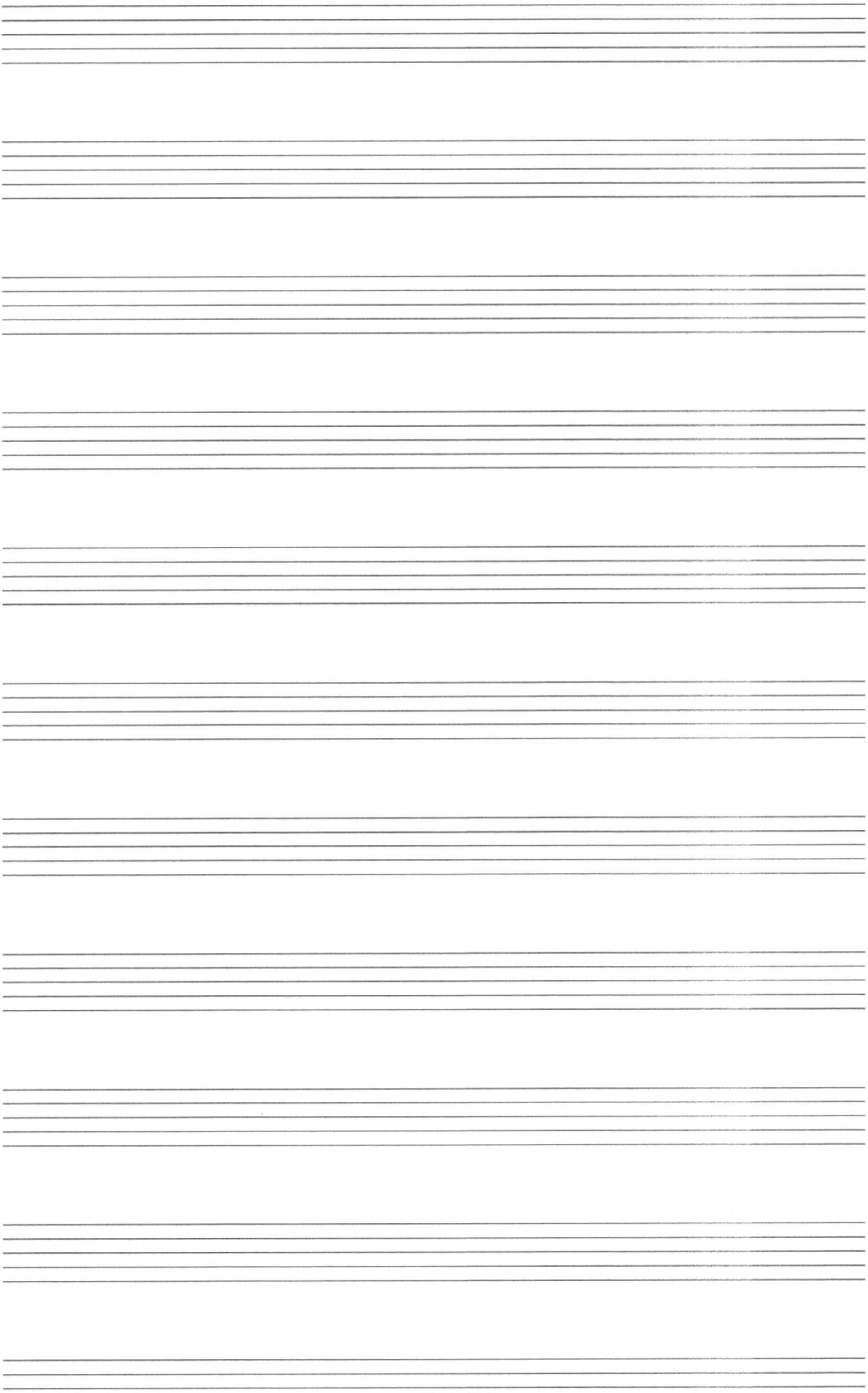

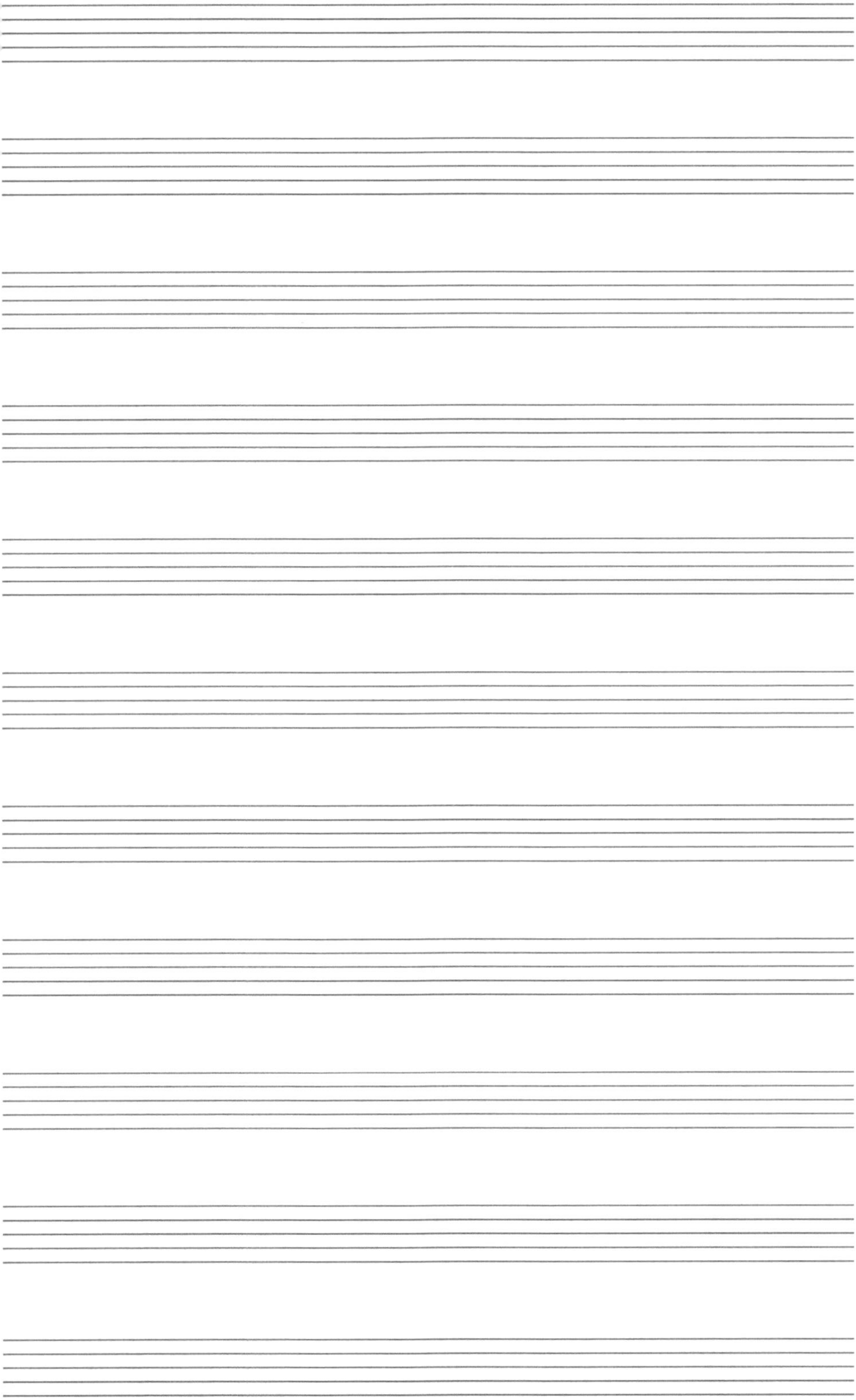

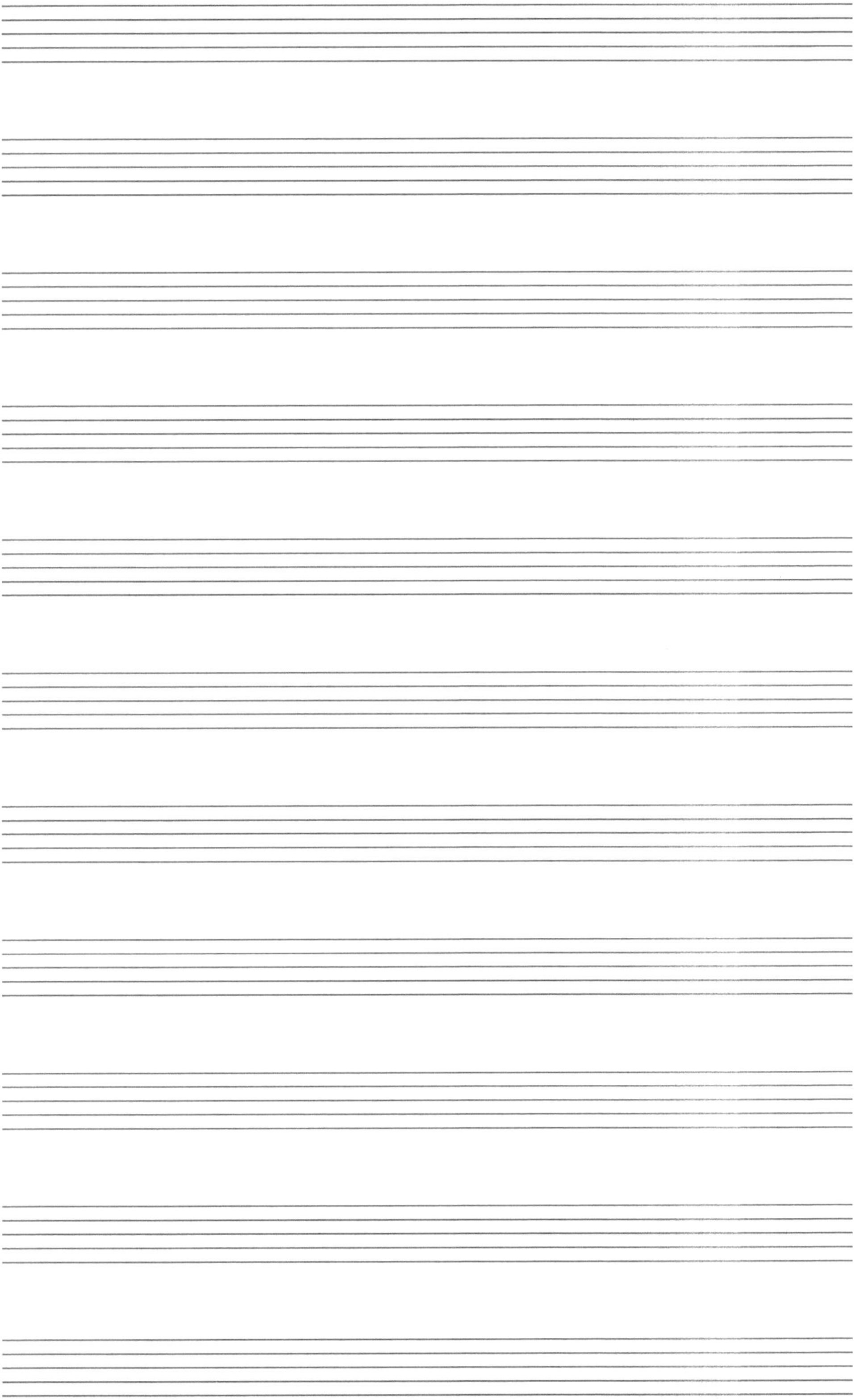

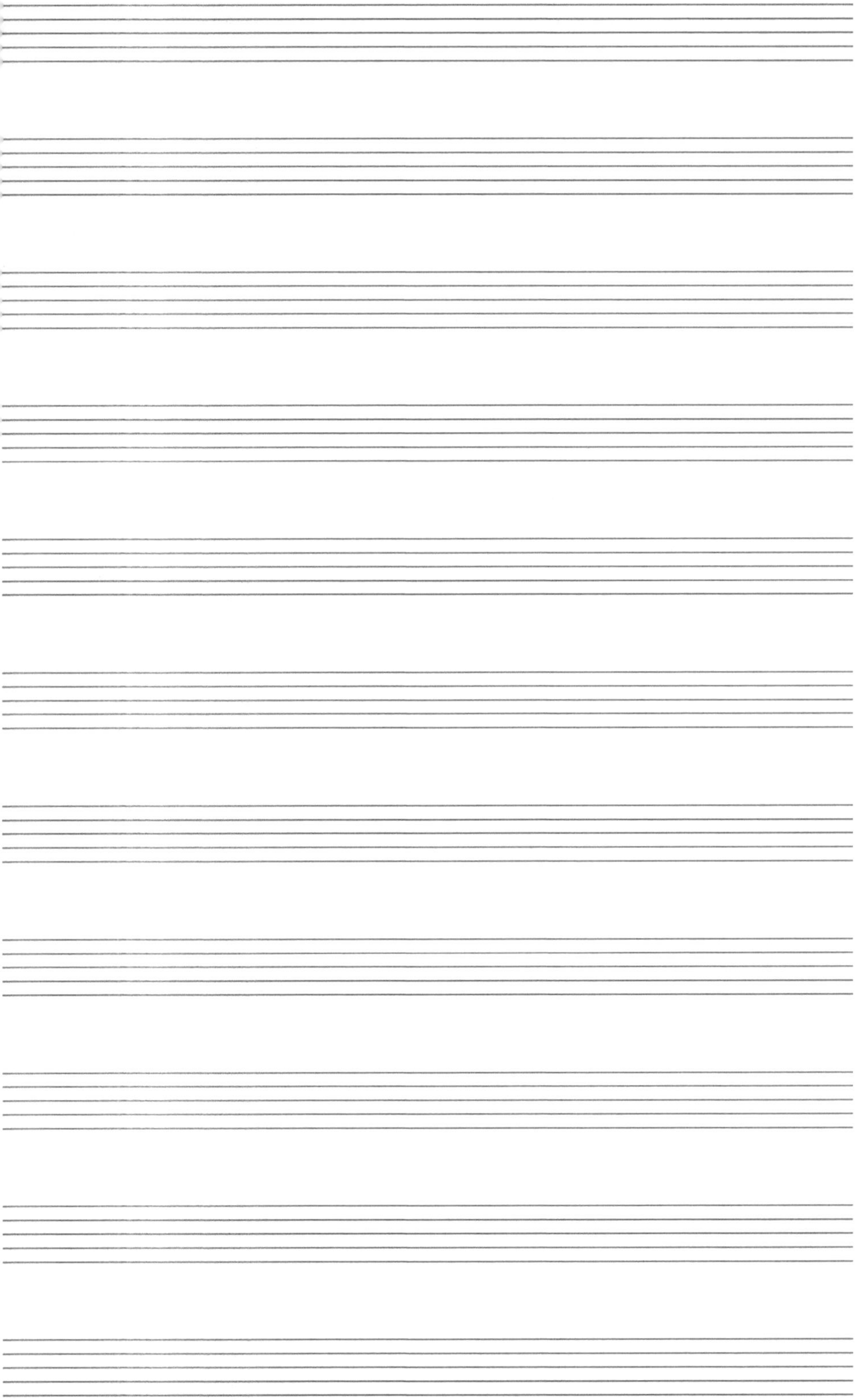

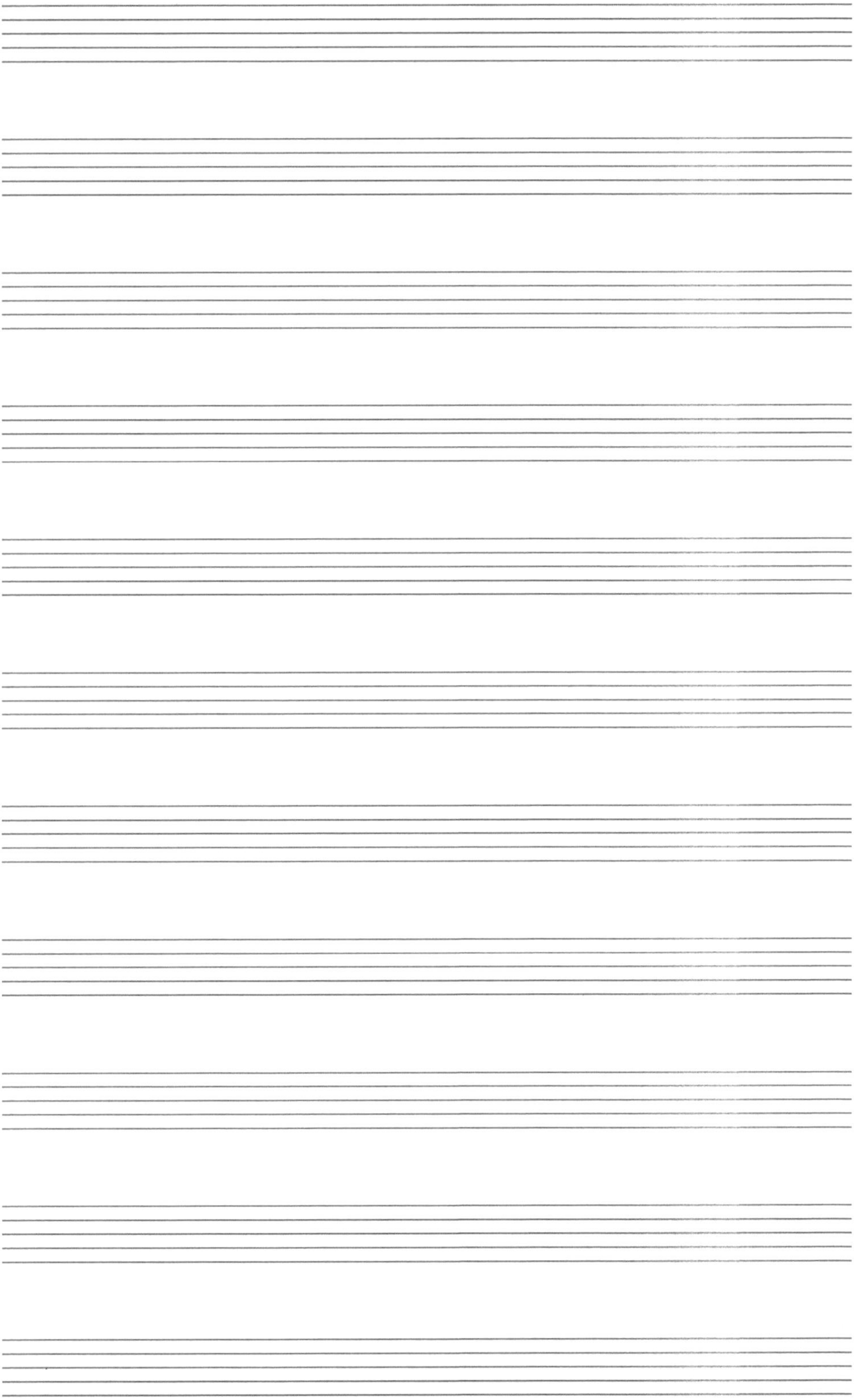

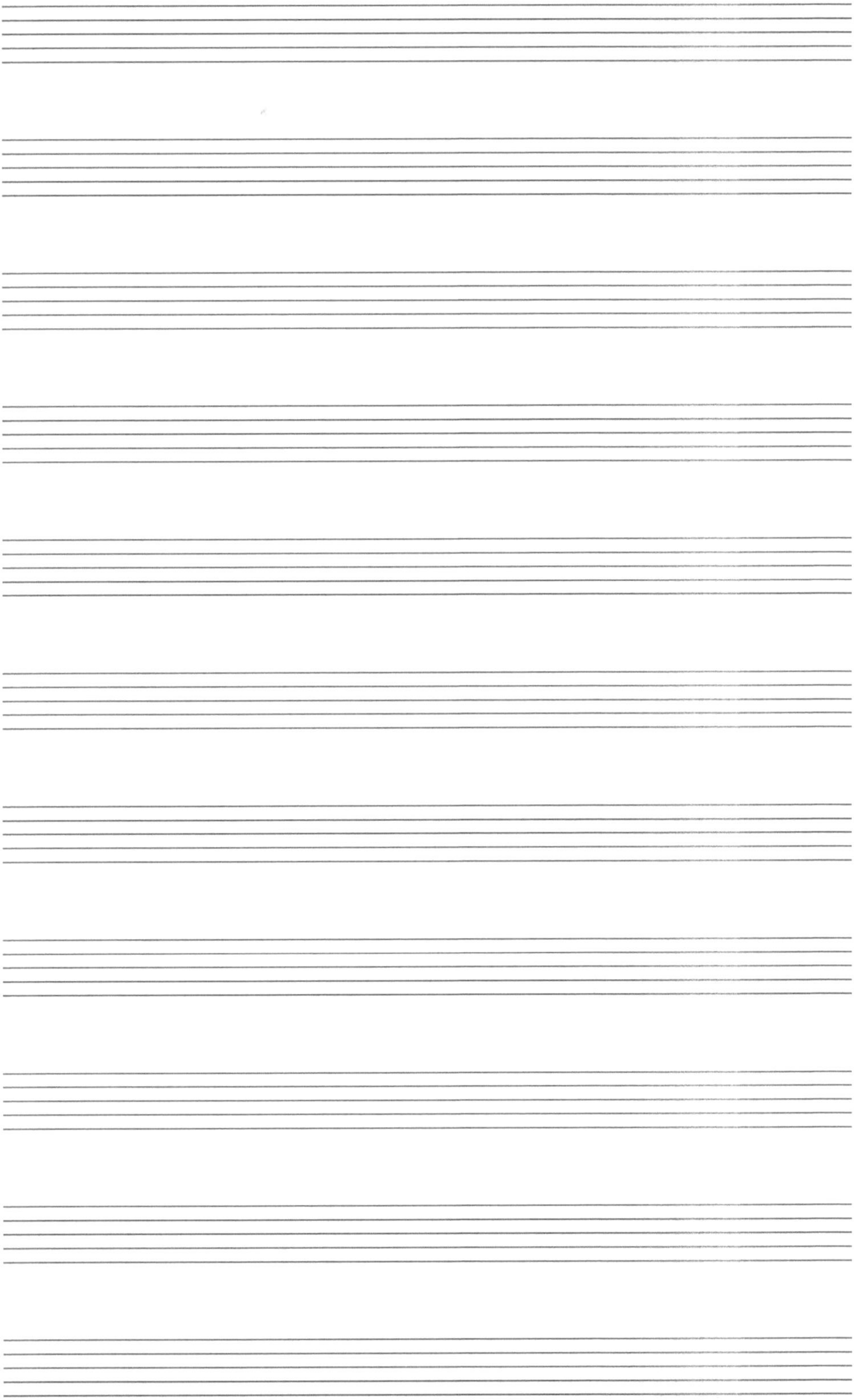

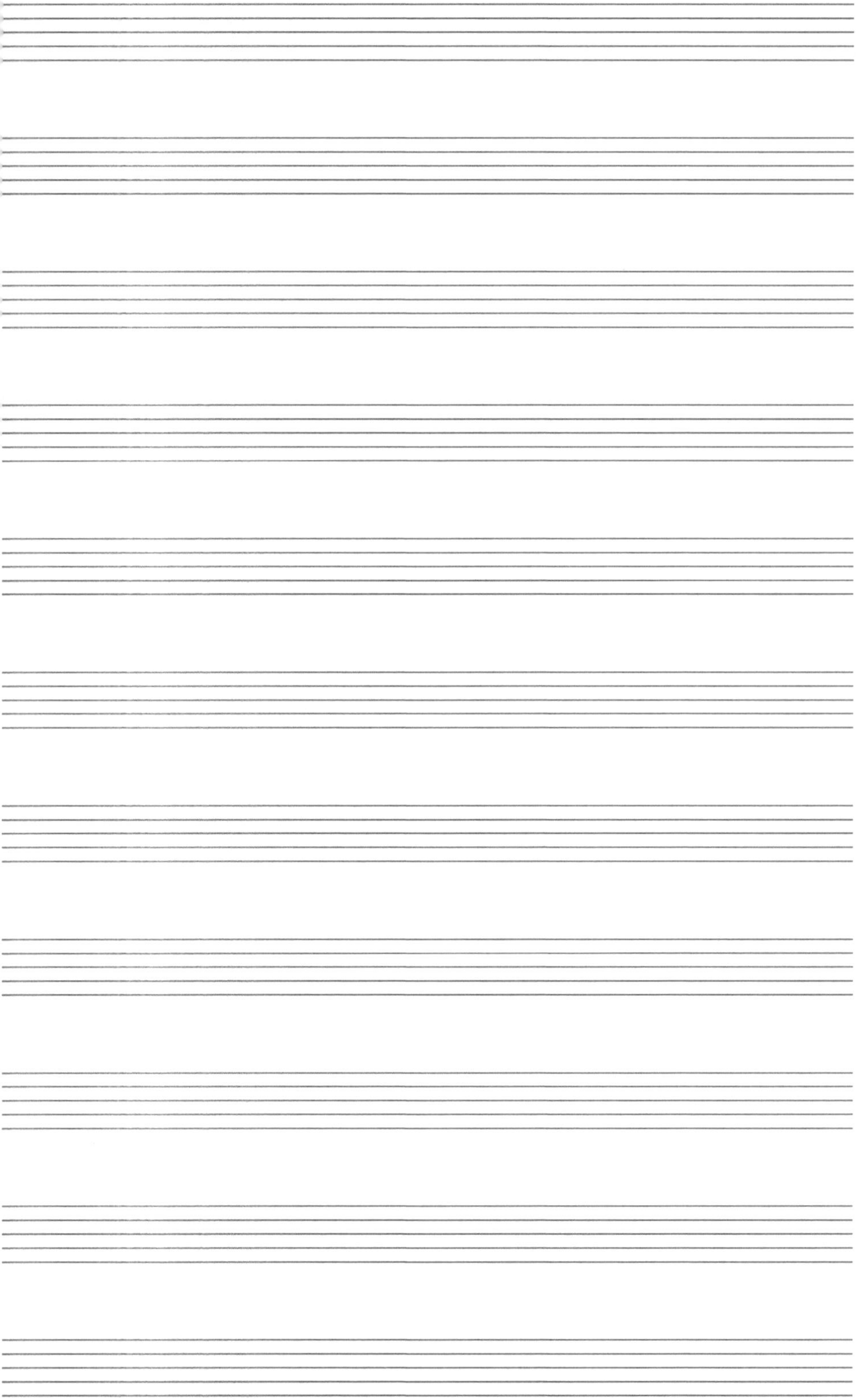

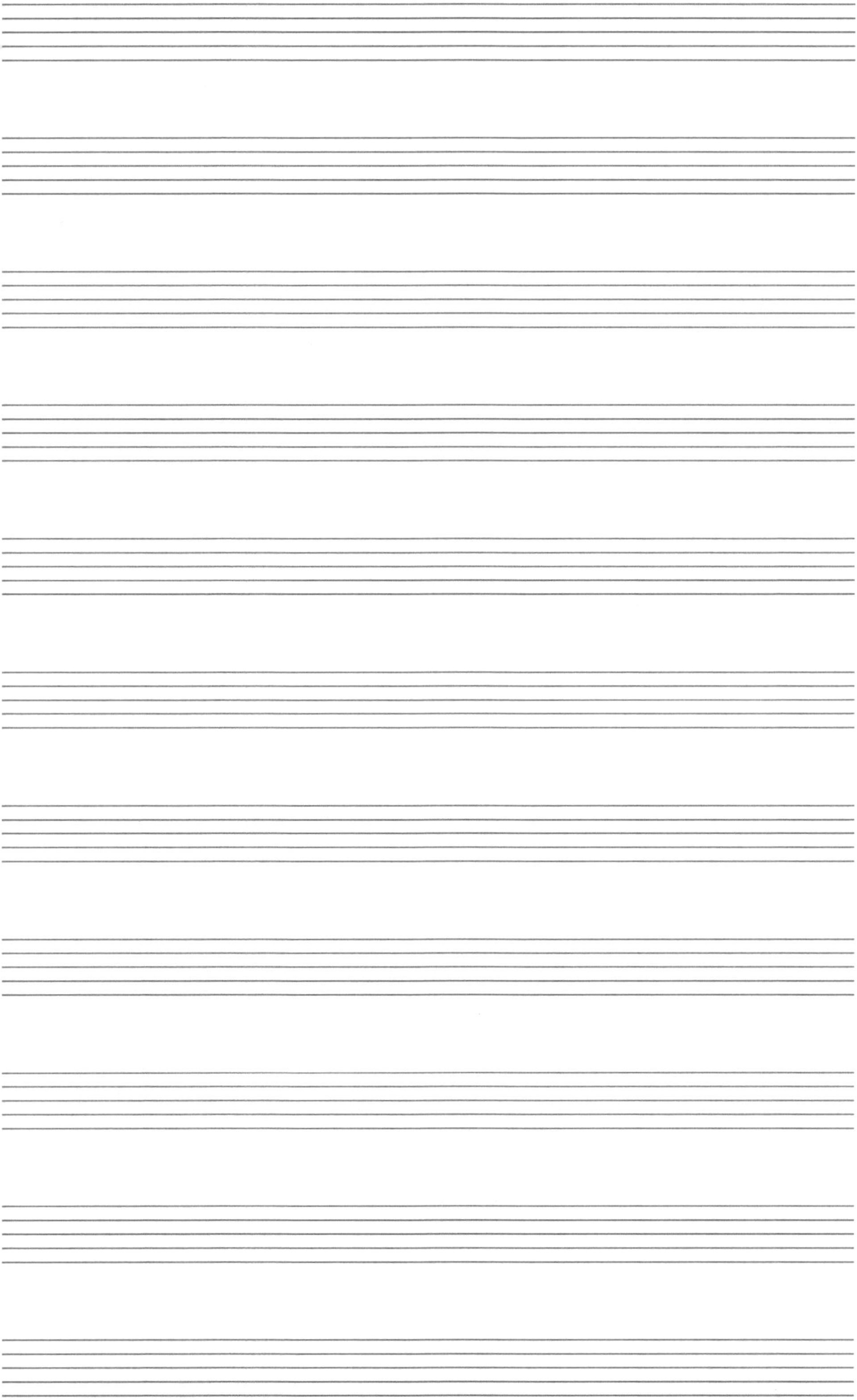

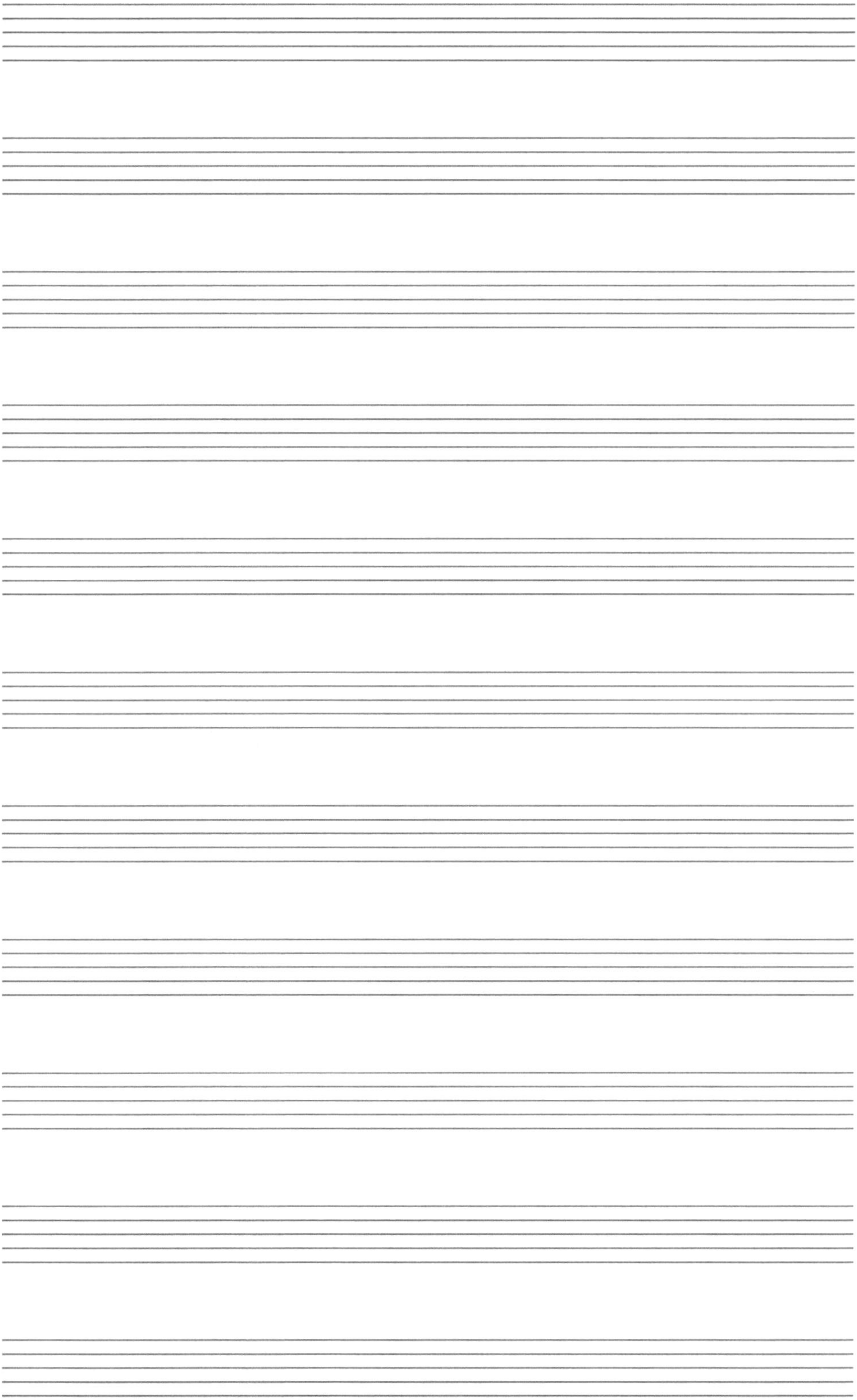

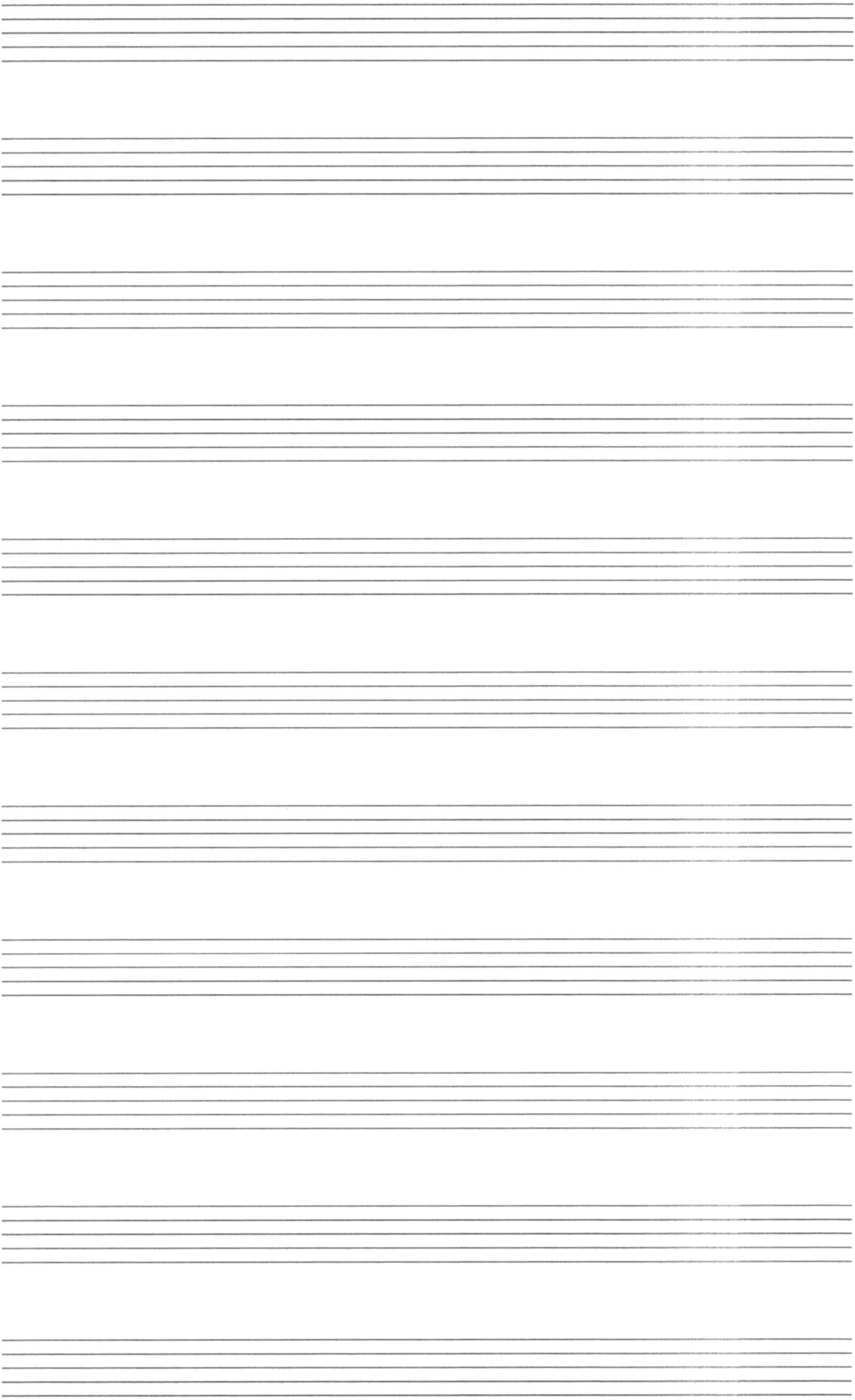

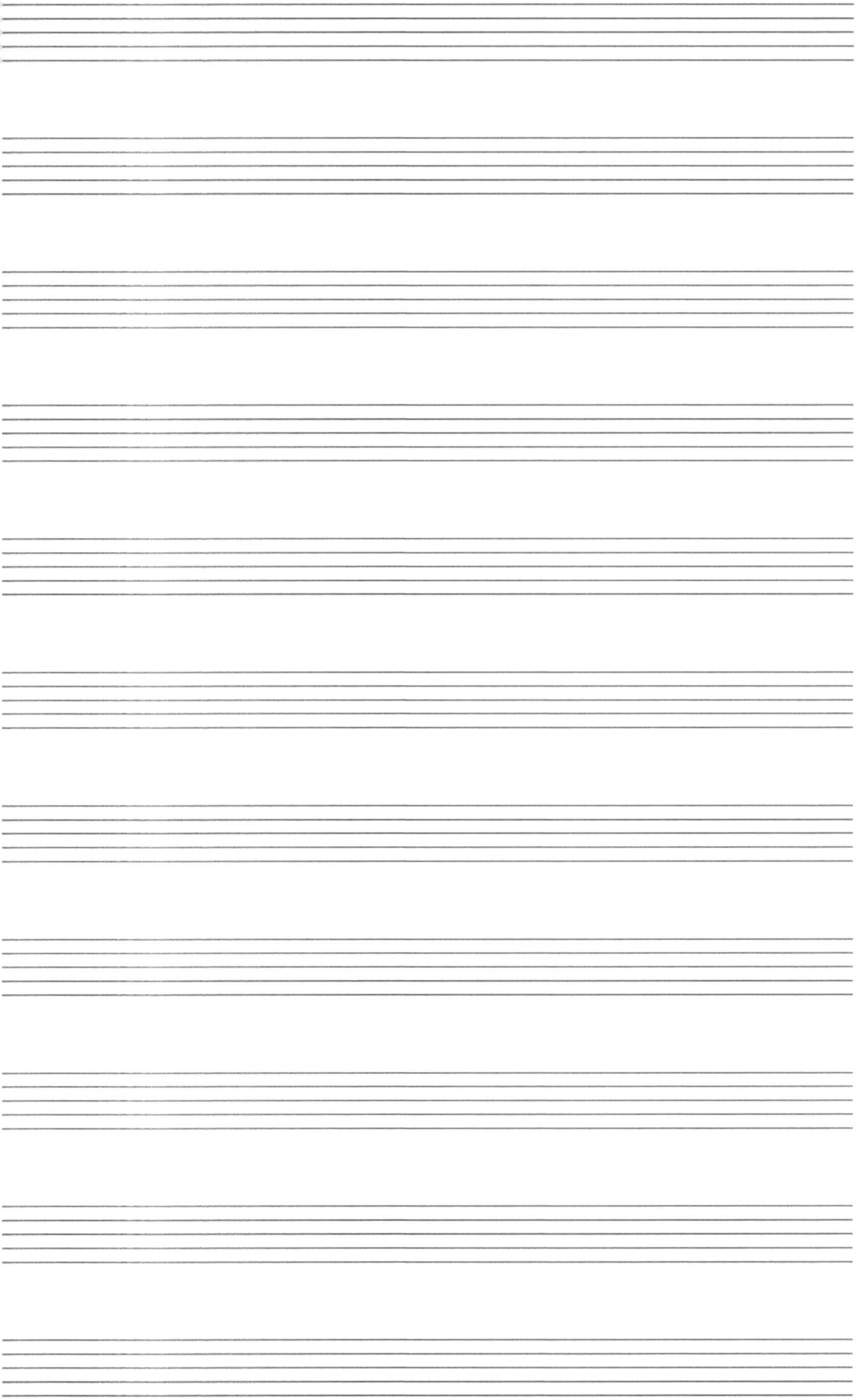

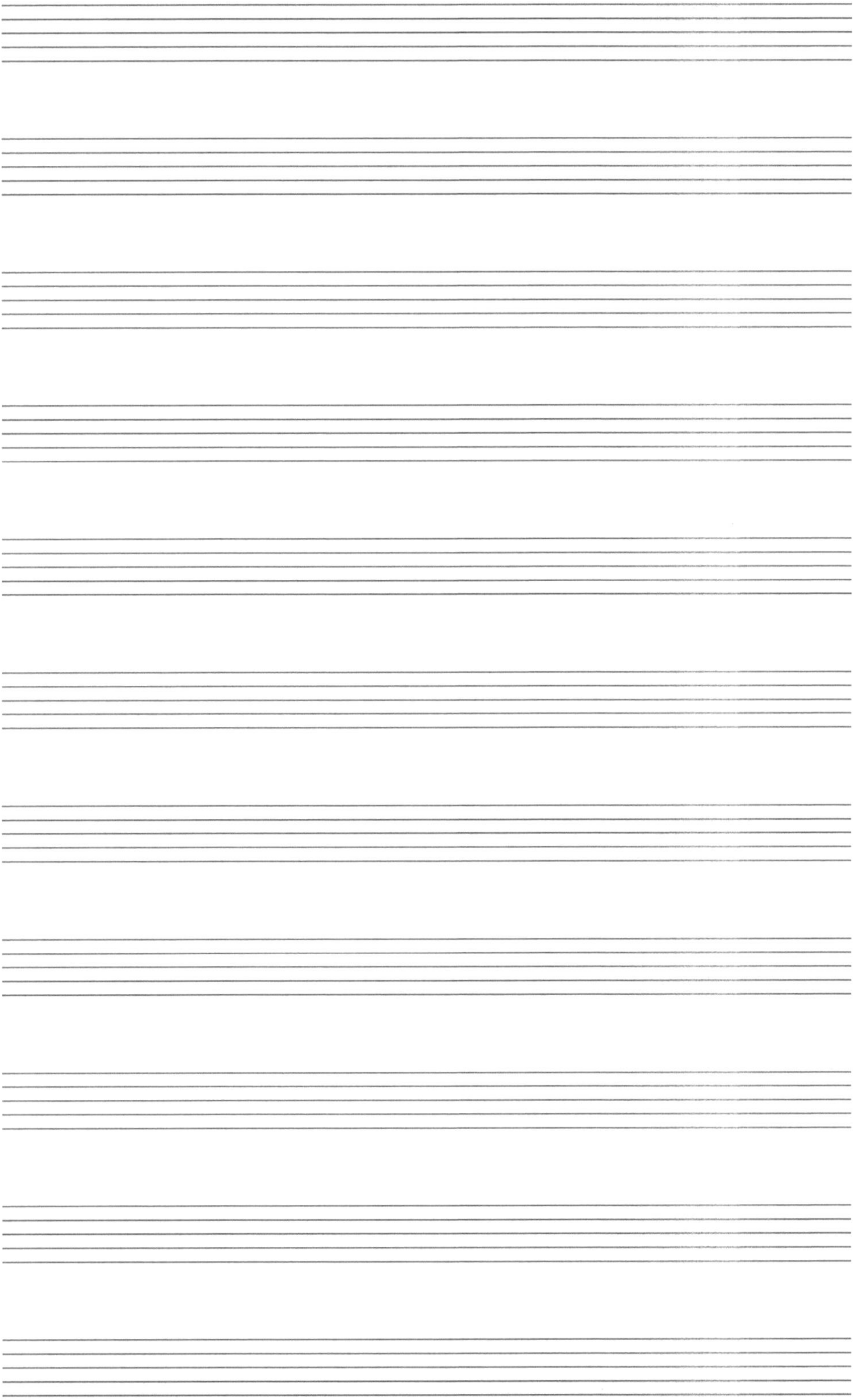

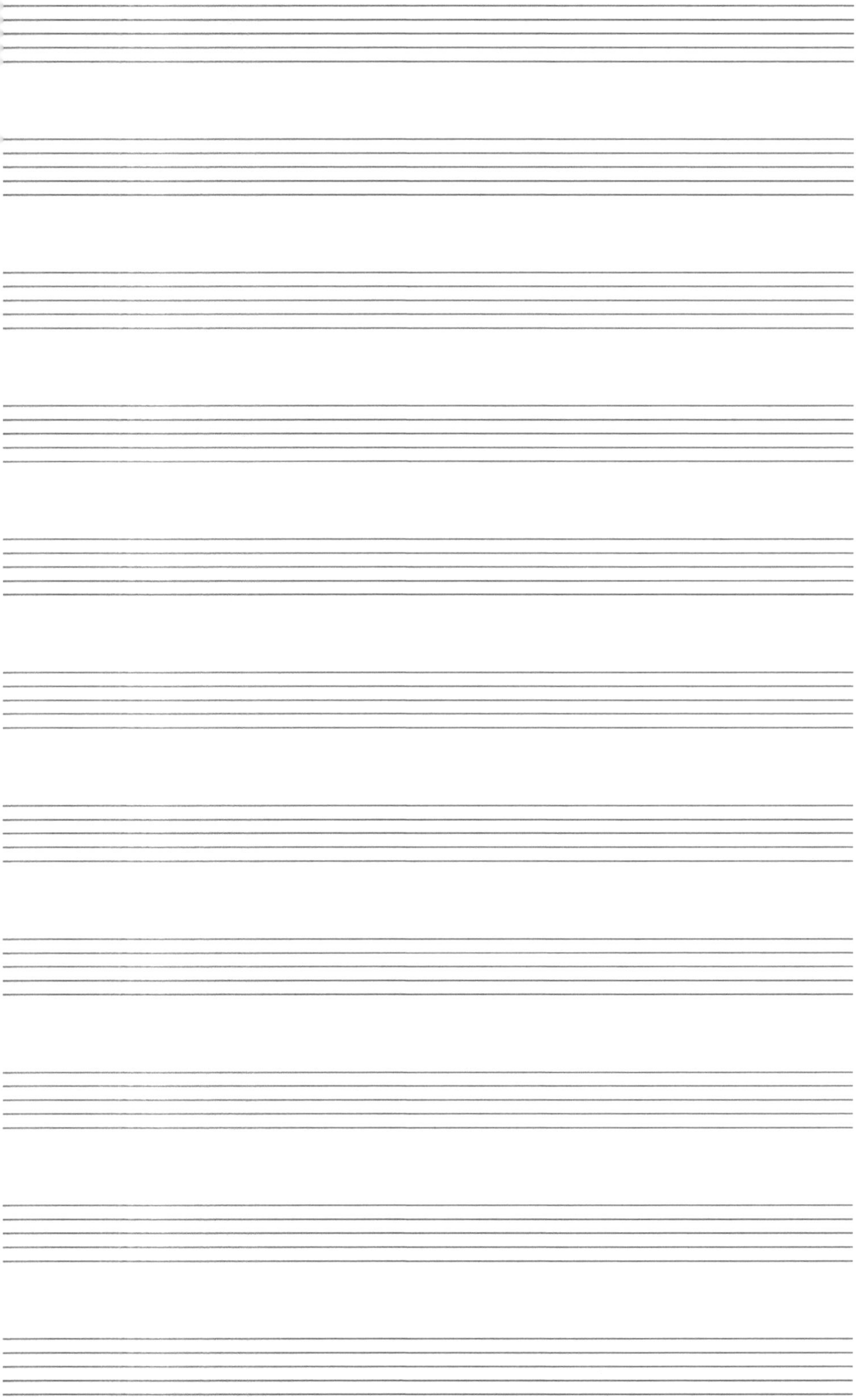

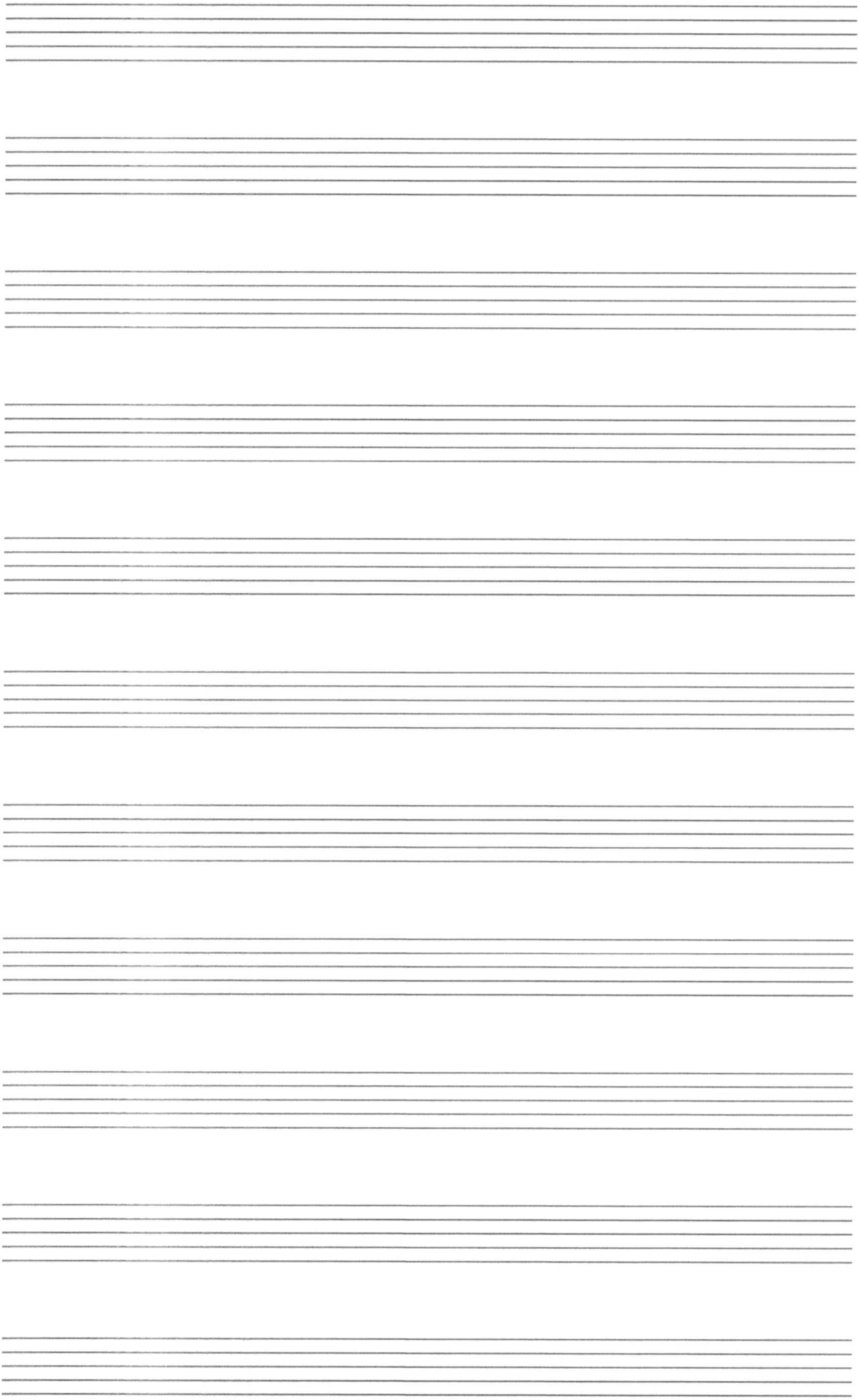

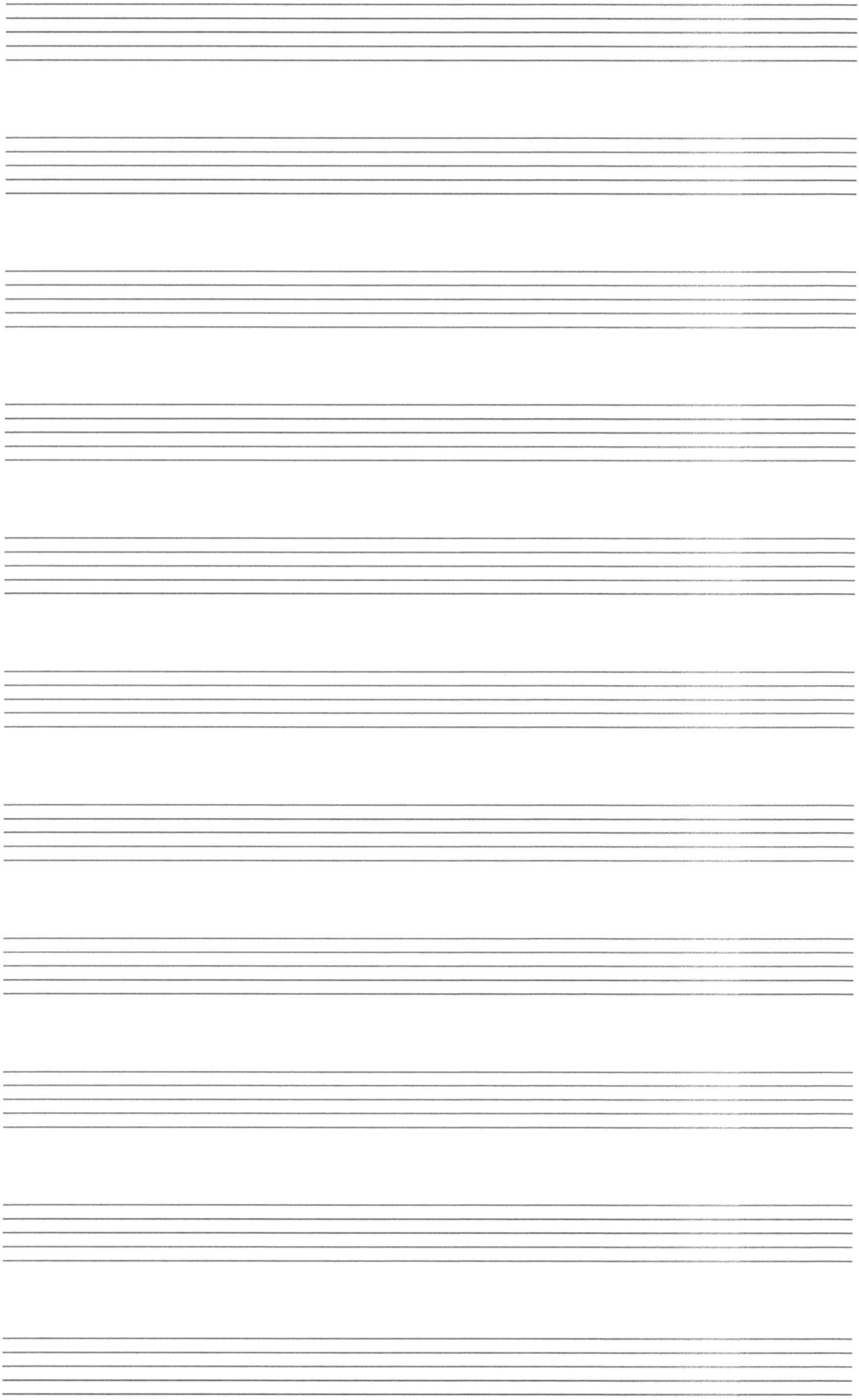

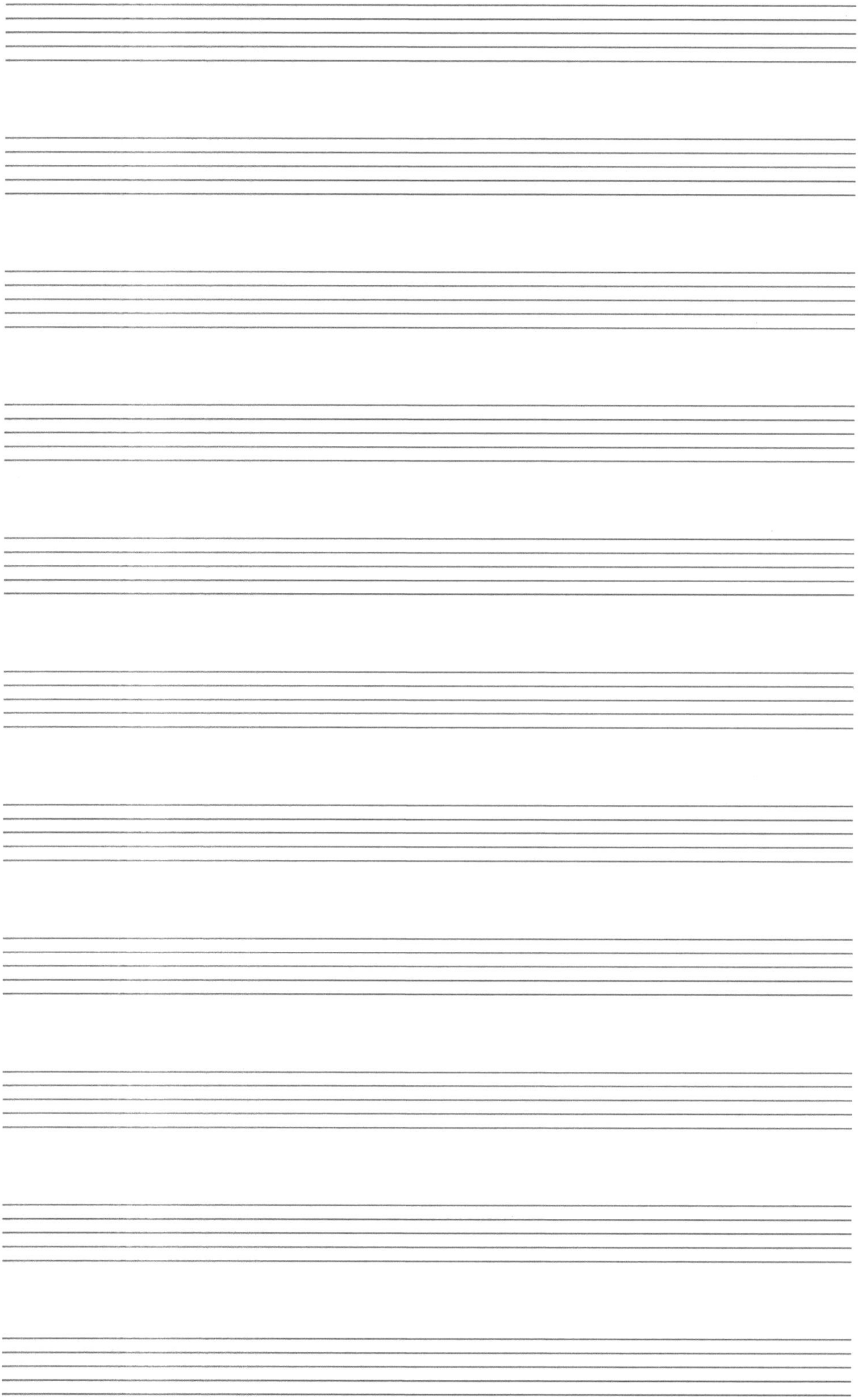

Made in United States
Troutdale, OR
04/21/2025

30780644R00066